California Studies in Food and Culture
—
DARRA GOLDSTEIN, EDITOR

ENCARNACIÓN'S KITCHEN

ENCARNACIÓN'S KITCHEN

—

MEXICAN RECIPES FROM
NINETEENTH-CENTURY CALIFORNIA

—

Selections from Encarnación Pinedo's
El cocinero español

EDITED AND TRANSLATED BY
DAN STREHL

—

WITH AN ESSAY BY VICTOR VALLE

UNIVERSITY OF CALIFORNIA PRESS   Berkeley Los Angeles London

Frontispiece: Encarnación Pinedo, ca. 1864.
(Photograph by H. Schoene, artist and photographer,
Santa Clara, California; reproduced courtesy of
Santa Clara University Archives.)

University of California Press
Berkeley and Los Angeles, California

University of California Press, Ltd.
London, England

Library of Congress Cataloging-in-Publication Data
Pinedo, Encarnación, b. 1848.
    [Cocinero español. Selections. English]
    Encarnación's kitchen : Mexican recipes from
    nineteenth-century California / edited and
    translated by Dan Strehl ; with an essay by
    Victor Valle.
        p.   cm.—(California studies in food and
    culture ; 9)
    Includes bibliographical references and index.
    ISBN 0-520-23651-3 (cloth : alk. paper)
    1. Cookery, Mexican. 2. Cookery—
California. I. Strehl, Dan. II. Title. III. Series.
TX716.M4 P553213   2003
641.5972—dc21   2002041379

Manufactured in Canada
12 11 10 09 08 07 06 05 04 03
10 9 8 7 6 5 4 3 2 1
The paper used in this publication is both acid-
free and totally chlorine-free (TCF). It meets the
minimum requirements of ANSI/NISO Z39.48–1992
(R 1997) (Permanence of Paper).♾

CONTENTS

ACKNOWLEDGMENTS

This reincarnation of Encarnación Pinedo has been aided by many people. Ruth Reichl, then at the *Los Angeles Times,* was the first to re-publish Pinedo's recipes, in an article on the history of California cuisine. Nohemi Carrasco Walker and her husband, J. Michael, have helped by checking my translations and clarifying traditional culinary technique. Master printer Vance Gerry published *The Spanish Cook,* a selection of Pinedo's recipes, in a fine-press edition from the Weather Bird Press. Victor and Mary Lau Valle and I have been discussing Pinedo for many years, and she was included in their *Recipe of Memory.* Joan Nielsen Castle scripted her into a *Too Hot Tamales* segment on the Television Food Network.

In Santa Clara, Charlene Duval, Sourisseau Academy for State and Local History, San Jose State University, gave good direction and intro-duced me to many local sources, including Bob Johnson at the California Room, San Jose Public Library. Anne McMahon, university archivist, Santa Clara University Archives, remarkably found Pinedo photo-graphs. Lorie Garcia, a historian in Santa Clara, was immensely help-ful and was a source of all things Berreyesa. Paula Jabloner, archivist at History San José, was also very helpful in providing photographs.

At the Huntington Library, Jennifer Watts found photographs, and Stephen Tabor helped decipher Encarnación's jumbled citations to early English books.

Special thanks go to Darra Goldstein of Williams College and Sheila Levine of the University of California Press for enthusiastically embracing the project and having endless patience with me.

And especially, thanks go to my wife, Romaine Ahlstrom. While at the Los Angeles Public Library and later at the Huntington Library, she chased down obscure references, graciously listened to Pinedo talk, tasted endless dishes, and continued to be encouraging long past reason.

Dan Strehl

A CURSE OF TEA AND POTATOES

The Life and Recipes of Encarnación Pinedo

—

VICTOR VALLE

There is nothing new in saying that cookbooks are read in bed or the garden as often as they are read inside the kitchen, for motives that have nothing to do with cooking. List all the cookbooks that have made the link between childhood memories and unsatisfied adult hunger, and you have filled a library with culinary nostalgia. But what about a recipe book that is intended to settle old scores, or one that is intended to protect its user from disappearing and doubles as a disguise from mortal enemies?

That, among other things, is what Encarnación Pinedo serves forth in *El cocinero español (The Spanish Cook),* a work of obvious importance for culinary historians. Published in 1898 in San Francisco, it is California's first, and clearly most extensive, Spanish-language cookbook. Anyone who reads Spanish and is lucky enough to get a copy of the thousand-recipe collection—you can find a copy in the Los Angeles Central Public Library—will discover a seminal text of Southwestern cuisine. Pinedo's *Cocinero* documents the start of California's love affair with fruits and vegetables, fresh edible flowers and herbs, aggressive spicing, and grilling over native wood fires. Her book also gives us California's first major collection of Mexican recipes, reason enough, it would seem, to translate and republish Pinedo's recipes. But recent scholarship suggests that she wrote more than just a memorable cookbook.

Pinedo and her book stand out in a time and place where men dominated the world of letters, and those letters were published in English. She was among that handful of nineteenth-century Latinas who published their works in the period following the conquest of Alta California. Moreover, Pinedo wrote exceptionally well, read and wrote in at least two languages, and received some formal education. Her literacy and education clearly mark Pinedo as a member of California's cultural elite.

A recent study by Rosaura Sánchez allows us to appreciate Pinedo's unique status. In her rereading of the nineteenth-century Californio testimonies collected by historian Hubert Howe Bancroft, Sánchez argues that his comprehensive history of California silences Mexican women in several ways. First, Bancroft allows the testimonies and histories written by Mexican, European, and American men to define Mexican female identity.[1] The American and European writers, for example, typically stressed the beauty and subservience of the Californio women, and the indolence and effeminate character of the Californio men, in order to justify taking "possession of both land and women."[2] Second, Bancroft and his collaborators collected fewer testimonies from female Californios. Third, although he utilized parts of their testimonies, he rarely identified them as sources. The silences he created gave him the liberty to fragment and reassemble their accounts in ways that suited his apologies for Manifest Destiny.[3] These silences also hid the individual voices of his informants. We know now that the female informants Bancroft's collaborators interviewed did not speak with one voice, but instead interpreted the conquest from different and sometimes conflicting political and social perspectives. At moments, their testimonies challenged the idea that Anglo conquest represented progress, and at other moments acquiesced to the new order. Bancroft's glosses, however, effectively suppressed the complexity of the female Californio testimonies for more than a century.

Pinedo's *Cocinero,* meanwhile, fell into obscurity despite her best wishes. In the *Cocinero*'s introduction, she addresses her subscribers, a clear indication of her efforts to defray the cost of publication. Like other nineteenth-century authors, Pinedo had sought advance sales of her book to demonstrate its sales potential to her printer, a Mr. E. C. Hughes. Judging from his publishing record, Hughes did not run a vanity press. The steam-driven press he operated in his shop published government and technical manuals, corporate bylaws, travel guides, commemorative speeches by visiting diplomats, and an occasional literary work.[4] Nevertheless, Pinedo's book suffered the fate of others written in a recently conquered language.

As a result, *El cocinero* and other seminal Californio texts languished in private libraries, while the life stories of other nineteenth-century Latinas collected dust in Bancroft's folios. For decades, few scholars thought to call upon these women as historical witnesses of the conquest and its aftermath. Instead, they preferred images of beautiful *señoritas* as objects of description. In recent decades, however, scholars from a number of disciplines have unearthed these nineteenth-century texts in an effort to reconstruct their voices. These efforts have yielded important cultural texts.

Published in 1885 in San Francisco, María Amparo Ruiz de Burton's novel, *The Squatter and the Don,* would be the first to retell California's conquest from a Mexican perspective. Written in English, her historical romance revisits the past in order to question "the 'American way' as a just, democratic and liberating system." Ruiz de Burton also subverted the negative Mexican stereotypes circulated by the Anglo press of her day. She created Mexican characters—though economically and politically subordinate—who were culturally and intellectually superior to their Yankee counterparts.[5] Pinedo's *Cocinero,* which was published in the same city thirteen years later, appears to have nothing in common with Ruiz de Burton's novel. It does not narrate a history; it does not create an imaginary world, or redress wrongs. It does not appear to be any more than it is—a book filled with culinary instructions, or so it would seem.

Scholars from various disciplines have now begun to read memoirs, letters, personal testimonies, and even cookbooks as literary texts rich in cultural meanings. Pinedo's *Cocinero* is simultaneously a book of recipes and identities. She shows us how her family dined, and how she reimagined her identity during a period of violent upheaval. By listing the ingredients of family recipes, she invoked the ghosts of a culture that was fast disappearing. By explaining how these ingredients were combined, she reconnected the fragments of her life, her individuality, and sense of feminine self-worth in a present filled with uncertainty. Pinedo's recipes can thus be read as testaments of hunger. She hungered for culinary and cultural continuity in a time of upheaval. Yet sating her special appetites depended upon her creative powers of memory and imagination. Through such an exertion of memory, she recalled the recipes of her childhood. The recipes she recorded summoned her past to the table. Once published, the recipes fixed her formulas for invoking that past, especially for family and friends who had not lived the glory of the *ranchos*. Pinedo, a custodian of memory, thus emerges as a precursor of such Latina memory artists as Denise Chavez, Maria Helena Viramontes, and Sandra Cisneros.

As with her literary descendants, however, her act of remembering was fraught with ambiguities and contradictions. Dead worlds revived by memory are not replicas of the past. They are interpretations riddled with gaps; the survivors fill in these gaps with their own inventions. These inventions of a past recreated in the present reveal much about the author's desires. The title of *El cocinero español* also betrays the author's desires. In her cookbook, she elected to bring aspects of her past to the foreground, while pushing others to the background.

Before Anglo conquest, Pinedo's ancestors had used the label of *gente de razón* (people of reason) to stress their status as Catholic settlers and to downplay their *mestizo* ambiguities. Among the racially mixed population of settlers, culture, religion, wealth, and regional loyalty counted more than skin color alone as social descriptors. Like other settlers in the borderlands, Pinedo's ancestors did not want to be confused with heathen *indios*. And by calling themselves Californios they stressed their local loyalties and their distance from the administrative centers of Guadalajara and Mexico City. But after conquest, Lisbeth Haas argues,

> That comparatively ample tolerance for color difference was not shared by the Anglo population, which had generally accepted a set of ideas about "white" racial superiority just prior to the Mexican War of 1846. After 1900, difference in terms of skin color superceded all other distinctions, and it became harder for Californios to negotiate a favorable status.[6]

While the new Anglo majority invariably racialized poor Californios by labeling them "Mexicans," some elite Californios insisted on calling themselves Spanish. Some chose this label because they believed it. Some elite Californios had fashioned their Spanish cultural identities before the Yankees arrived, while others deployed the label to pass as second-class whites. Some Anglos were inclined to accept the *ranchero* elite as honorary whites, and ignore antimiscegenation laws, if doing so brought them land, money, or higher social status. European Americans "were not oblivious to the advantages of marrying into wealthy *ranchero* families," writes historian Tomás Almaguer. "With eligible white women being scarce in the territory, fair complexioned, upper-class Mexican women were among the most valued marriage partners available."[7] Few Californio women could have matched the social prestige of the women in Pinedo's family tree. Not surprisingly, many of the women of Pinedo's generation and social station used their family names and reputations, real or embellished, to marry into the new Anglo elite. As Pinedo's family history reveals, a woman's decision to marry the conqueror often provoked a sense of bitterness, disappointment, and betrayal among her immediate relations.

On June 28, 1846, at San Rafael in the northern borderlands of Alta California, a group of Bear Flag rebels led by Kit Carson noticed a small boat in which a pair of teenage boys rowed an older gentleman toward shore. José de los Reyes Berreyesa, one of California's wealthiest ranchers, had just crossed San Francisco Bay with his two nephews, Francisco and Ramón de Haro. He had traveled north from San Jose to find his son, who, at that moment, was jailed in Sonoma for allegedly conspiring against the rebels, an allegation that was later proved false.[8] Carson intercepted the party, suspecting them of spying. He had been instructed by Major John C. Frémont to take no prisoners, an order he interpreted with perverse literalness. Carson gave the signal to fire. Some accounts report that Carson's men fired upon Francisco and Ramón as they rowed to shore.[9] The Berreyesa descendants, however, say the men executed don José's nephews after they had disembarked.[10] Both accounts agree that the sixty-one-year-old don José then flung himself over the bodies of the young boys, asking Carson's men why they had not taken his life instead. They promptly obliged don José's request.[11]

Eight years later, in a bid to take control of the New Almaden Mine—a fabulously rich mercury deposit that soon proved invaluable in refining the Gold Rush ore—a gang of hooded men lynched Nemesio Berreyesa, don José's son. By 1856, Yankee miners and vigilantes had lynched or shot eight Berreyesa men, including the brother, named Encarnación, of Pinedo's mother, María del Carmen Berreyesa. Crooked lawyers and squatters also beset the family's 160,000 acres of Santa Clara Valley land. And so it went until this family, once one of the most land-rich among Californio families, lost everything. Broke and mired in litigation, the seventy-member clan had no choice but to beg the San Jose town government for a small plot on which to build new homes. The family blamed treacherous Yankee lawyers, freebooters, and squatters for robbing and murdering them, and the Mexican government for failing to protect their vast holdings. To other disillusioned Californios, the Berreyesa tragedy came to symbolize the measure of their collective defeat.[12]

For Encarnación Pinedo, that decade must have seemed a netherworld in which a dying past coexisted with a hostile future. Pinedo, the daughter of María del Carmen Berreyesa, was born May 21, 1848, a year before the second onslaught of Yankee miners into California. She lived close enough to her past to invoke its presence, and long enough to see its decline.[13] At age fifty, a spinster living upon her married sister's generosity, she preserved her family's recipes even as the world to which they belonged was ending. She began her book with a dedication to her nieces: "So that you may always remember the value of a woman's work, study this volume's contents."[14] Her dedication does not mention that her nieces married Anglo men. The omission disguises the dual nature of her gift: the recipes would not only contribute to their domestic happiness, but her descendants would also use these formulas to transmit the Californio half of their newly hybridized cultural identities to another generation.

Pinedo builds her bridge to the past without mentioning her family's persecution and material losses. I believe her evasions have a strategic function. In an article written in 1901 for Santa Clara's *Sunday Bulletin,* she relates her family's role in developing the New Almaden Mine, but without mentioning Nemesio's lynching. She merely notes that "the Government of the United States took possession of the mine," a version of events that neither asserts nor contradicts her family's claims.[15] Years later, the Berreyesa family accused Major Frémont of ordering their uncle's murder. They insisted that the men he commanded had killed Nemesio to force Nemesio's wife into selling their ranch.[16]

One of the last surviving members of the Berreyesa clan said she understood Pinedo's silences. Naomi Berreyesa, who was ninety-two years old when I interviewed her, said her family feared their tormentors. "My great-grandfather was afraid his family was going to get it next. That's why he said to his family, 'Let's go back to Mexico.' Even to this day, we have been treated like criminals," she said, referring to her fruitless efforts to persuade the government to acknowledge the legality of her family's land claims. "You wonder why my blood boils over. There are still family members who feel this way."[17]

And felt that way in Pinedo's day as well, judging by María del Carmen's order forbidding her daughters to talk to Gringos, whom she still blamed for killing Pinedo's grandfather and uncles.[18] Yet Pinedo would see her sister and six of her nieces defy her mother's wishes and marry Yankee men.[19] Surely, Pinedo sensed the disappointment and betrayal these marriages provoked in the elder Berreyesas. Surely, her mother and relatives reminded her that she bore the name of an uncle lynched by the Yankees. Her aunt Engracia, for example, refused to forgive Carson's men for killing her father. This is how she recounted the story of José's murder to a reporter: "When my mother heard the news of my father's death she fainted. . . . The Gringos were a bloodless people. They lived on tea and potatoes."[20] Tellingly, Engracia used a culinary insult to denounce those whom she believed to be as soulless as their cooking.

Pinedo echoes her aunt's disdain for Yankee cooking, but with more refinement and with a flair for condescension. In the *Cocinero*'s introduction, Pinedo casts Latinized Catholics, not Protestant Yankees, in the leading culinary roles. She conveys this idea by foregrounding her recipes with a culinary history that begins in classical antiquity, implicitly claiming Lucullus and Apicius as her culinary forerunners. She also notes the debt French cooks owed to Italian cuisine, and the superiority of French culinary technique above all others.[21] Pinedo, in other words, by presenting her recipes as a continuation of a classic tradition, places her cuisine in the culinary mainstream, which for her was Catholic Europe. Pinedo stressed her Catholicity as her ancestors had. She belonged to *la gente de razón*. Then she turns a scornful eye upon the English:

> The English have advanced the art a bit, enough that several of its writers have published on the subject: a Mr. Pegge in 1390, Sir J. Elliot in 1539, Abraham Veale in 1575, and Widovas Treasure in 1625. Despite all this, there is not a single Englishman who can cook, as their foods and style of seasoning are the most insipid and tasteless that one can imagine.[22]

Pinedo's mention of a book attributed to a Widovas Treasure, which does not appear to exist, suggests that her knowledge of these texts came from hearsay. Still, the level of her culinary gossip should not come as a complete surprise, if one considers Pinedo's education and the company she kept. At the Notre Dame Academy in San Jose, she came under the influence of a northern European convent culture with a cosmopolitan outlook that valued bilingualism. As a day student she studied under French- and Flemish-speaking nuns, some with European university degrees, who taught the academy's elementary through high-school curriculum.[23] As with other Catholic orders established in

California after 1848, the academy had introduced bilingual instruction to further their "Americanization" program.[24] The arrival of forty-
two Guatemalan nuns in 1859 further enhanced the academy's multi-
lingual atmosphere, and these nuns may have tutored Pinedo on the
fine points of literary Spanish.[25]

Given her family history and schooling, the absence of Yankee
recipes in her cookbook makes sense. Her omissions seem to express
a refusal to acknowledge those who had turned her world upside down.
Read today, her subtle arrogance may seem charming. She counted
herself among the civilized. Her culinary inclusions and exclusions
show how she constructed herself as a civilized subject, one, contrary
to the myth of ethnic victimhood, who relegated Anglos to the position of barbarous Other. But does the *Cocinero*'s title mask a paradox:
did she knowingly stress her Spanish heritage at the expense of her
Mexican cuisine, or did her title express omissions that jibed with an
identity she had never thought to question? My guess is that Pinedo,
in the act of remembering, chose to revise her past to remove any
doubts about the provenance of her recipes. Even if she had not ques-
tioned her Spanish identity while growing up, the act of publishing
recipes that traced their origins to Mexicans, via their culinary texts
and memories, must have forced the identity question into her con-
sciousness. Her choice may have been a pragmatic decision to make
her book more salable, a desire to put her identity above any racial
suspicion, or perhaps both. Her descendants had faced this ambigu-
ity before.

Her Californio ancestors claim that the Berreyesas came from the
Basque region of Spain in 1731 to what is now the northwest Mexican
state of Sinaloa. Fifteen-year-old Nicolás Antonio Berreyesa, Pinedo's
great-grandfather, then joined the de Anza California expedition of
1775–76.[26] The church archives in which the families that joined the

expedition are registered tell another story about the family's origins. These records categorized the majority of those trekking northward as members of mixed-race castes. Miraculous transformations then occurred upon arrival in the northern borderlands. They were now far enough away from officialdom to drop their caste titles and become *gente de razón*. These name changes did not alter one crucial fact. Most of California's settlers were *mestizos* and Christened Indians, with a sprinkling of Asians and Africans. Few of the settlers were actually Iberian immigrants. Moreover, the act of taking Indian, *mestiza*, and African wives and adopting indigenous traditions, customs, and foods further naturalized these Spaniards to the so-called New World during the three-hundred-year-long process of moving up from Mexico. This was Hispanic America's paradox of conquest. In the act of expanding their empire, the native conditions and cultures gradually transformed the Spaniards and their institutions. Our present-day knowledge of the conquest thus requires the reader to look beyond the *Cocinero*'s title to understand the context in which Pinedo lived and cooked her cuisine.

My colleague Dan Strehl did not see any ambiguities in the *Cocinero*'s literary genealogy. After a thorough reading of rare Mexican culinary texts, Strehl concluded that Pinedo's recipes are the descendants of Mexico's nineteenth-century cuisine, which, with its "distinctive Spanish, Indian, and French influences," provided a sophisticated contrast to the amateur cookbooks compiled by the wives of the first Anglo settlers.[27] These recipes clearly suggest the influence of Mexican texts. Pinedo's *mole de carnero,* or lamb *mole,* for example, is a virtual word-for-word copy of a *mole caraqueño de carnero* (Caracas-style lamb *mole*) recipe in a Mexican cookbook published by Simon Blanquel in 1853.[28] Although adapted to her local circumstances, many of Pinedo's recipes are variations of Mexican themes or Spanish standards previously incorporated into the Mexican canon. She had multiple opportunities to collect these recipes: from a formidable extended family, from the academy's Guatemalan nuns, from the Mexican cookbooks advertised in California's Spanish-language newspapers, and from recipes clipped from the Spanish-language illustrated magazines of her day. Whatever the sources, Pinedo's Mexican recipes are preceded by Spanish-sounding names. But her *aves en mole gallego* (fowl in a Galician *mole*), *guajolote en clamole* [sic] *castellano* (turkey in Castilian *clemole*), and *guajolote en mole gallego* (turkey in Galician *mole*) are just simplified versions of Mexican originals.[29] (The words *mole* and *clemole* are both derived from the Nahuatl word for "sauce"; *guajolote* [turkey] is another example of Mexican Spanish with a Nahuatl root.) A few recipes acknowledge Mexican influences with terms such as *a la mexicana,* while others, such as Pinedo's *lengua enchilada* (tongue in chile sauce), build upon Mexican cooking concepts and ingredients.[30] Still, Pinedo does not acknowledge a source for the *mole*-like sauce in this recipe, which begins with toasted, dried California chile, sesame, and almonds ground to a crunchy texture, or for her other recipes that borrow terminology, ingredients, or cooking techniques from Mexican sources.

Her recipes show more than a grasp of ingredients and cooking techniques. In contrast to some nouvelle chefs today, who often travel the one-way street of subjecting native ingredients to European cooking methods, Pinedo's interpretations demonstrate a mastery of both European technique and *mestizo* aesthetics, an achievement rarely matched by subsequent Anglo interpreters of Mexican cooking. But why Hispanicize the names of Mexican recipes or disguise the fact that her "Spanish" cooking was inextricably rooted in Mexican cuisine? Was she simply acting upon an artist's prerogative to rename recipes? Most likely, Pinedo, like other elite Californio women, preferred the term *español* because it designated elevated social status. She expressed that status by creating a culinary context for her recipes, one that meshed with the social and political context in which she wrote and published them.

I believe Pinedo used her recipes to create a new identity for herself, one that allowed her to recover some of her family's former dignity. She did this by incorporating Mexican cuisine into her Spanish self, thereby appropriating Catholic European respectability in an attempt to improve her position in relationship to the more powerful Anglos who surrounded her. Pragmatic considerations, such as the blatant racial discrimination against the poorer and darker Californios, probably motivated the renegotiation of her identity. The writing and publishing of recipes represented one of the rare ways a woman of her time might earn money by respectable means. The success of Helen Hunt Jackson's popular novel *Ramona*, published fourteen years earlier, may have alerted Pinedo to the marketing potential of romantic Californio themes. As a spinster living with her sister's Yankee husband, her status—and perhaps her income—as an author also may have helped her to deflect any suspicion of abusing her brother-in-law's generosity. The same goes for her immediate social circle. Emphasizing her Spanish past allowed her to maintain her place in elite society while racism increasingly dominated the public sphere.

Californio antagonisms with Mexican civil authority also may have influenced her loyalties. Mexican nationalism may have arrived too late to change her loyalties, but it's hard to say for sure. We can only judge her by what she wrote, which reveals quite a lot. "Silver-toned bells come with the light of the Gospel all the way from Old Spain," she wrote in a newspaper article, invoking her recent past as a Spanish idyll graced by beautiful *señoritas* and gallant *caballeros*.[31] In the same article, she perpetuates the brutal myth that California Indians enjoyed the floggings given them by the *padres*. "Obedience from the Indians was enforced by flogging," she wrote. "When an Indian looked sad and they asked him what was the matter with him he would answer that he was sad because he missed his flogging and upon getting one he would say: 'Now I am warm and satisfied.'"[32] My hunch is that she found it easier to embellish a lie than to denounce it. Perhaps retelling the story helped her ease her guilt. After all, the Anglo newcomers frequently pointed to the *ranchero*'s mistreatment of Native Americans as proof of Mexican tyranny. At least, that is how Mexican-Americans who came of age politically during the 1960s once judged Pinedo's generation. But I wonder how our generation would have held up under the same circumstances?

Unfortunately, the contradictions expressed by Pinedo and her peers helped a new governing majority construct racial identities for California's Mexican population. A hard, unforgiving line now divided what had been a heterogeneous community with a loosely defined ethnic and racial identity. Scores of cookbook writers and journalists followed her lead. By the 1930s, the concept of Mexican food had become so thoroughly Hispanicized that only astute observers could note the irony of ordering tamales and enchiladas in a "Spanish" restaurant.

Pinedo may have been the first Californio writer to participate in the culinary formulation of Spanish romance, but she wasn't the last. During the early twentieth century, the Anglo majority's increasing fascination with romantic Old Spain also imprisoned native New Mexican cookbook writers such as Fabiola Cabeza de Baca Gilbert within its socially acceptable definitions of Mexican identity. Cabeza de Baca could only publish her book, *The Good Life: New Mexico Traditions and Food,* if she stayed within the bounds of majority cultural expectations. These concessions resulted in debilitating contradictions. Genaro Padilla argues that the native New Mexican writers of Cabeza de Baca's generation engaged in "intense cultural self-deceit, political fear, and masked and self-divided identity" to appeal to an audience dominated by the colonizing majority.[33]

However, excessive supplication to majority taste could be unsettling. The dominating culture suppressed the discomfort of witnessing the minority culture's awareness of its "masked and self-divided identity" by erasing their memories of conquest and by representing their domination as social progress. Representing conquest as progress required that the conquerors symbolically include the precolonial elite in their power structures. Pageants and fiestas often provided the opportunity for bestowing ceremonial positions of authority upon the defeated elite. In time, the defeated internalized the lie and transported their tragic history to "a fabulous domain of cultural romance, aristocratic pretense," and, Padilla notes, "self-deceit."[34]

Fortunately, the fantasy was not entirely convincing. In moments of reflection, members of the defeated elite acknowledged the reality of their degraded status, which emboldened some to subvert the myths that sustained their make-believe authority. If you listen carefully to these New Mexican writers, you can hear a native cultural "I" cursing the bars of the cultural prison in which the imperial "Other" has confined them.[35] The *Cocinero*'s dismissal of English cooking and its exclusion of Yankee recipes show Pinedo rattling her prison bars more than three decades before her New Mexican sisters would attempt the same. Despite her contradictions, she asserted her existence, and did so proudly, at a time when history conspired to erase it. Her Spanish identity also gave Pinedo a weapon to resist cultural effacement. The romance of her cuisine continually invoked a past that predated the time of her defeated present. By encouraging friends and family to taste the pleasures of that time, she could reveal to them the authentic "natives" in their midst.[36] As Padilla observes: "We no longer have a recipe book of quaint 'Spanish' recipes, but a gesture of cultural assertion."[37] The act of creating a culinary legacy for succeeding generations thus expresses self-love in the face of denigration, and faith in the possibility of some day reestablishing a lost cultural continuity. That day appears to be drawing near as Mexican culture, now urban and transnational, regains its former centrality in public and private life.

Notes

1. Rosaura Sánchez, *Telling Identities: The Californio Testimonios* (Minneapolis: University of Minnesota Press, 1995), pp. 188–90.
2. Ibid., p. 200.
3. Ibid., p. 28.
4. A search of the WorldCat database conducted on November 18, 1999, turned up twenty-four works in which Hughes is listed as a San Francisco printer or publisher.
5. María Amparo Ruiz de Burton, *The Squatter and the Don*, ed. and intro. by Rosaura Sánchez and Beatrice Pita (1885; reprint, Houston: Arte Público Press, 1992), p. 7.
6. Lisbeth Haas, *Conquests and Historical Identities in California, 1769–1936* (Berkeley: University of California Press, 1995), p. 10.
7. Tomás Almaguer, *Racial Fault Lines: The Historical Origins of White Supremacy in California* (Berkeley: University of California Press, 1994), p. 59.
8. Sánchez, *Telling Identities*, p. 265.
9. Leonard Pitt, *The Decline of the Californios: A Social History of the Spanish-Speaking Californians, 1846–1890* (Berkeley: University of California Press, 1966), pp. 30–31.
10. Sánchez, *Telling Identities*, p. 265.
11. Pitt, *Decline of the Californios*, p. 30.
12. Ibid., 102–3.
13. Dan Strehl, ed. and trans., *The Spanish Cook: A Selection of Recipes from Encarnación Pinedo's "El Cocinero Español"* (Pasadena, Calif.: Weather Bird Press, 1992).
14. Encarnación Pinedo, *El cocinero español: Obra que contiene mil recetas valiosas y utiles para cocinar con facilidad en diferentes estilos* [*The Spanish Cook: A Work Containing a Thousand Valuable and Useful Recipes to Cook with Ease in Different Styles*] (San Francisco: Imprenta de E. C. Hughes, 1898), p. 3.
15. Encarnación Pinedo, "Early Days in Santa Clara," *Sunday Bulletin*, June 9, 1901, p. 1.
16. Pitt, *Decline of the Californios*, p. 102.

17. Naomi Berreyesa, telephone interview by Victor Valle, September 1992.

18. Mrs. Fremont Older [Clara Baggerly], "The Pathfinder's Victim," pt. 2, *San Jose Mercury*, ca. 1925.

19. Mrs. Fremont Older [Clara Baggerly], "William Fitts' Omnibus," *San Jose Mercury*, ca. 1925.

20. Older, "The Pathfinder's Victim."

21. Pinedo, *El cocinero español*, pp. 5–8.

22. Ibid., p. 6; my translation.

23. Day-student experience: Older, "William Fitts' Omnibus"; characteristics of nuns: Eduardus J. Hanna, *In Harvest Fields by Sunset Shores: The Work of the Sisters of Notre Dame on the Pacific Coast* (San Francisco: Gilmartin Company, 1926), pp. 32–33, 198.

24. Almaguer, *Racial Fault Lines*, p. 63.

25. Arrival of nuns: Hanna, *In Harvest Fields by Sunset Shores*, p. 196; nuns tutoring Pinedo: Sister Julie Bellefeuille, archivist for the Sisters of Notre Dame de Namur, telephone interview by Victor Valle, Saratoga, Calif., September 1992.

26. Marie Northrop, *Spanish American Families of Early California, 1769–1850*, 2 vols. (Burbank: Southern California Genealogical Society, 1976, 1984). "Berryessa" is the modern spelling of the family name. "Berreyesa" and "Bereyesa" were used during the eighteenth and nineteenth centuries.

27. Strehl, *The Spanish Cook*, p. 1.

28. Simon Blanquel, *Novisimo arte de cocina; o, Excelente colección de las mejores recetas* (Mexico City: Imprenta Tomás Gardida, 1853).

29. Pinedo, *El cocinero español*, pp. 24, 113.

30. Ibid., p. 145.

31. Pinedo, "Early Days in Santa Clara," p. 2.

32. Ibid.

33. Genaro Padilla, "Imprisoned Narrative? Or Lies, Secrets, and Silence in New Mexico Women's Autobiography," in *Criticism in the Borderlands: Studies in Chicano Literature, Culture, and Ideology*, ed. Héctor Calderón and José David Saldívar (Durham, N.C.: Duke University Press, 1991), p. 43.

34. Ibid., p. 44.

35. Ibid.

36. Ibid., p. 54.

37. Ibid., p. 55.

IN ENCARNACIÓN'S KITCHEN

DAN STREHL

A century ago, Encarnación Pinedo produced a landmark of American cuisine, *El cocinero español: Obra que contiene mil recetas valiosas y utiles para cocinar con facilidad en diferentes estilos. Comprendido advertencias y explicaciones aproposito que ponen el arte de la cocina al alcance de todos (The Spanish Cook: A Work Containing a Thousand Valuable and Useful Recipes to Cook with Ease in Different Styles. Including Advice and Explanations That Put the Art of Cooking within Reach of Everyone)*, published in San Francisco by E. C. Hughes, in 1898. The first cookbook written by a Hispanic in the United States, it was also the first recipe-specific recording of Californio food, Mexican cuisine as prepared by Spanish-speaking peoples born in California. The Californios painfully lost their cultural and political dominance after the United States acquired California, and Pinedo made the only published record of this remarkable cuisine. Her book gives us the first and only contemporary account of how Mexican food was prepared in California during the nineteenth century. But because the book was written in Spanish, it is generally unknown today.[1]

Encarnación Pinedo

The Spanish Cook goes significantly beyond being just a cookbook. It is a sociological document that serves as a testimony of a lost culture. Pinedo is particularly important, as she was a woman, Hispanic, and has a personal history that can be reconstructed, unlike the vast majority of cookbook writers. As a group, nineteenth-century Latinas were marginalized in society and generally omitted from the historical record. Pinedo was both educated and left a record. We have this record because of her family's dramatic history. Pinedo was a third-generation Californio, whose family roots were firmly planted among the earliest settlers of northern California.

Pinedo's great-grandfather was Nicolás Antonio Berreyesa, who arrived in the San Francisco Bay Area with the de Anza expedition of 1775–76. He was married to María Gertrudis Peralta. Their son José de los Reyes Berreyesa was born January 6, 1785, at Santa Clara, and he became a sergeant at the San Francisco presidio. When he retired, he received a grant for the Rancho San Vicente from Governor Alvarado in 1842. The rancho's forty-four hundred acres encompassed what was to become the New Almaden Mine, a long-term source of tragedy and litigation for the family. In 1805, José married María Zacarias Bernal at the Mission Santa Clara. Her family had occupied the Rancho Santa Teresa as early as 1826.[2] José and María had eight children. Their daughter María del Carmen was baptized on February 4, 1811, at the Mission Dolores. Several of their children died in tragic circumstances during the American conquest of California. José was murdered by Kit Carson on Major John C. Frémont's instruction on June 28, 1846.

Encarnación's father, Lorenzo Pinedo, arrived in California from Ecuador, the sole survivor of a shipwreck off the coast at Monterey.[3] After he had established himself, he married María del Carmen Berreyesa, daughter of José de los Reyes Berreyesa, on August 25, 1839, at Mission Santa Clara. They had two children: Dolores, born April 29, 1845, and Encarnación, born May 21, 1848.

In 1842, Lorenzo Pinedo received a land grant to the eleven-thousand-acre Rancho Las Uvas, located about three miles west of today's Morgan Hill. In 1845, Lorenzo asked for and received from Antonio Pico a grant for the land outside the mission. He built the first house in the town of Santa Clara, on the lot bounded by Santa Clara and Market Streets and Alviso and Lafayette Streets. The first residence outside the Mission and *ranchería* (settlement), it was unusual in that it was a wood-frame house made of redwood, instead of the usual adobe construction. Pinedo had the redwood cut in the Santa Clara mountains and brought to the settlement. The house stood until about 1915. Encarnación and Dolores grew up there, in the atmosphere of the expansive hospitality of the extended Berreyesa family. The proximity of the house to the Mission, about two blocks away, meant that it became the site of most of the funeral vigils held for the Californio community of Santa Clara during the 1850s and 1860s, and the family had a reputation for being excellent hosts.[4]

Lorenzo died suddenly of cholera at the end of November 1852.[5] He had gone to visit the Rancho San Vicente, and there became a victim of an epidemic. He dictated his will on his deathbed, leaving his property to María del Carmen, with the provision that she take "special care for the education of my children."[6] He named as his executor James Alexander Forbes, a relative of Carmen's by marriage. Forbes was a somewhat disreputable character (for example, when he sold a mansion he built for eleven thousand dollars to an order of nuns, he neglected to mention that it had a twenty-thousand-dollar lien on it), but he was an accepted part of the family. One of Forbes's lasting achievements was the construction of a flour mill in nearby Los Gatos.[7]

Encarnación, only four years old when her father died, may have followed a Mexican tradition, as portrayed in Laura Esquivels's novel *Como agua para chocolate (Like Water for Chocolate),* in which the youngest daughter remains single in order to care for her widowed mother. In 1874 María del Carmen deeded her property to Encarnación, and María died August 11, 1876, when Encarnación was twenty-eight. In Mexico at that time women were candidates for marriage at the age of fourteen. By age thirty, a woman was considered a spinster. Nonetheless, Encarnación was described as "a woman of beauty and popularity. She kept alive the spirit of the old days of Santa Clara."[8]

Encarnación's sister, Dolores, married a man named William Francis "Billy" Fitts, who was born near Bangor, Maine, on October 9, 1837. His parents, Elijah T. and Emeline E. (Gilmore) Fitts, moved to Massachusetts when he was a baby, and they came to Santa Clara in 1852 via the Isthmus of Panama.[9] A Captain Ham had founded an omnibus line between Santa Clara and San Jose in the late 1850s. Fitts was a driver for Ham, and started his own line in 1861, the Accommodation Line Omnibus, the first horse-drawn carriage service between Santa Clara and San Jose. It ran from Cameron House in Santa Clara to Auzerais House in San Jose. He transported many young women from Santa Clara to the convent school at Notre Dame Academy in San Jose.[10] Eventually he became romantically involved with one of the passengers, Dolores Pinedo. The deaths of so many Berreyesa family members at the hands of the Anglos had left long and bitter memories in the Berreyesa family, and the children had been forbidden by María del Carmen to talk to Anglos. Nonetheless, Dolores married the Anglo Fitts in about 1864 against the wishes of her family. Dolores and William moved next door to the Pinedo family residence on Aliso Street. They had eleven children: Ida, Angelina, Erminia, Leticia, Carmencita, William, Luna, Charles, Lena, Carmelita, and Arturo.

At some point, probably after the death of María del Carmen but before the 1880 census, Encarnación was living in the Fitts household. Her book was written for and dedicated to her nieces to enable them re-create a cuisine that was vanishing in their own homes. She managed to express her disdain for the Anglos by mocking their recipes, such as ham and eggs, with a satirical title: *huevos hipócritas*. As Victor Valle shows in his introduction, Pinedo used the politics of culinary incorporation and exclusion both to contest and to acquiesce to California's postcolonial Anglo domination.

Fitts's omnibus business lasted until 1869, when he joined the San Jose and Santa Clara Railroad Company as an operator of their horse-cars, a job that would last a number of years. From 1876 to at least 1879, he was town marshal of Santa Clara.[11] When the electric trolley cars came in, he was made the superintendent of the railway from 1883 to 1890.[12] Eventually, he became a jailer in San Jose and moved to that city. After a four-year term as jailer, he went to work for the San Jose Water Works, until he retired in 1914, at the age of seventy-seven. He died two years later, on March 14, 1916. Encarnación died April 9, 1902, at fifty-three years of age. Dolores Fitts died November 1, 1909, at the age of sixty-four. The three of them are buried side by side in the Oakhill Cemetery in San Jose.

Mexican Culinary Traditions and Literature

Pinedo's book is remarkable in that it appears to be the first juncture of Mexican and Californian culinary publishing traditions. While England and France developed a significant body of culinary literature beginning in the sixteenth century, Iberia did not. France, for example, published at least 255 cookbooks between 1650 and 1789,[13] but there were relatively few titles published in Spain and Portugal prior to the nineteenth century. John Super estimates there were about 8 culinary titles in the first 350 years of printing in Spain, and even fewer titles in Portugal.[14] However, early Spanish cookery books came to Mexico and were popular there: cookbooks from Spain were available for sale in Mexico as early as 1584.[15] Among the most common works were Diego Granado's

Libro del arte de cocina (1614), Juan de Altamiras's *Nuevo arte de cocina* (1758), Francisco Martinez Montiño's *Arte de cocina, pastelería, vizcochería, y conservía* (1725), and Juan de la Mata's *Arte de repostería* (1747).

In Mexico, recipe transmission historically has been from mother to daughter in the course of the child's domestic training. The tradition of recording recipes in written form has its origin in the late eighteenth century.[16] A number of these manuscripts have survived, and in the twentieth century several were published.[17] The majority of the extant ones were written in convents, as opposed to those written for the home. Nuns were active in culinary practice and frequently recorded their recipes. The most famous of these, though not the most extensive, is the *Libro de cocina del Convento de San Jerónimo,* attributed to one of the greatest Mexican authors of the seventeenth century, Sor Juana Inés de la Cruz.[18]

In Mexico, the printing of cookbooks began in the 1830s, with large comprehensive books authored mostly by men. By that time Mexico possessed a highly evolved cuisine combining distinctive Spanish, Indian, and French influences. This is documented in the first cookbook printed in Mexico, in 1831, *El cocinero mexicano. El cocinero mexicano* has had a remarkably long and important life in Mexican culinary literature. In 1845, the 1834 edition was rearranged in alphabetical order by Mariano Galván Rivera and published under the title *Diccionario de cocino; o, El nuevo cocinero mexicano en forma de diccionario.* Subsequent versions were published throughout the nineteenth century, with reprints through the twentieth century.

Perhaps thirty or more cookbook titles were published in Mexico during the nineteenth century. Jeffrey Pilcher cites fifteen in the appendix to his dissertation, "*Vivan* Tamales: The Creation of a Mexican National Cuisine," but the bibliography of Mexican cookery is still very incomplete. Some of these nineteenth-century titles were available in the California market and must have been seen by Pinedo. Her education had exposed her to a significant knowledge of early cookery literature, and she displays a clear sense of the context in which she was writing. It is interesting to note that the first cookbook printed in Mexico that named a woman as the author, Vicenta Torres de Rubio's *Cocina michoacana*, was published in 1896, only two years before Encarnación's work was printed.[19]

Two Spanish-language cookbooks were printed in the United States before Pinedo's book appeared. The first, *Arte nuevo de cocina y repostería, acomodo al uso mexicano*, is cited as being published in 1828 by the Casa de Lamuza, Impreseores Libreros, New York.[20] The second was the *Novisimo arte de cocina; o, Excelente colección de las mejores recetas*, published in Philadelphia in 1845 by the Compañía Estereotipográpfica de la América del Norte, also for the Mexican market.[21] This was a slightly expanded version of *Nueva cocinera mexicana; o, Excelente colección de las mejores recetas*, published in Mexico City by Luis Heredia in 1841, which made at least one other appearance, under the same title, in 1853, when it was published in Mexico by Simon Blanquel.

California's Culinary Literature

English-language cookbooks first appeared in California in the 1870s, some twenty-five years after the Anglo acquisition of the state. The first, about 1870, was the *Peerless Receipt Book*, a promotional pamphlet for baking soda. But the vast majority were charitable cookbooks from Episcopalian and Methodist cooks, showing off the fine points of the white Protestant cooking that had originated in the northeastern United States. In 1872 the first of these appeared: *The California Recipe*

Book; How to Keep a Husband; or, Culinary Tactics; and The Sacramento Ladies' Kitchen Companion.

The California Recipe Book was produced by the Ladies of the First Congregational Church of San Francisco. This church had been founded in 1849, during the Gold Rush. In May 1872, a new church building was dedicated. The San Francisco Bulletin said that it "rivals the best in America . . . walls of red brick, surmounted by a spire which rises 225 feet from the sidewalk . . . with a pew capacity of 1600." Where the income (if any) from the cookbook went is unclear, but we can surmise that it went to the building fund.

The Sacramento Ladies' Kitchen Companion was produced by the Ladies of Grace Church and published by H. S. Crocker, "Steam Printer." (Crocker's publishing house is still in business today.) A new church was built in 1871, at a cost of twenty-six thousand dollars, with a ten-thousand-dollar mortgage. By 1874, the congregation had fallen behind on the mortgage, and the church went bankrupt in 1877. Lacking more information, one would guess that the church's mortgage (or the sixteen thousand dollars paid up front) may have come in small part from the efforts of the Ladies of Grace Church.

There is no explicit claim of authorship for How to Keep a Husband, but the advertisements suggest that it was produced by an Episcopal church, of which there were several in San Francisco at the time.

The California Recipe Book and the Sacramento Ladies' Kitchen Companion are similar in size, with 45 and 40 pages respectively, and with 160 and 154 recipes. How to Keep a Husband was considerably larger, at 76 pages with 200 recipes.

About one hundred more titles were published in California during the nineteenth century, and recipes from exotic foreign cuisines appeared in a few. The books were typically small, averaging less than one hundred pages, and limited in their coverage, focusing on baking and desserts. Pinedo's book was one of the largest and most compre-hensive works printed in nineteenth-century California. Her liberal use of spices, chiles, vinegars, and wines provided a striking flavor con-trast to the bland recipes offered by other texts.

Pinedo's book is unique and important in that there were no other books printed that contained such a large number and variety of Mexican recipes. The few Mexican recipes that did appear in other books were often contributed by Anglo women. *Cooking Receipts: Good in Their Way,* published about 1901, contained about forty Mexican recipes, the recipes' signatures clearly indicating the class position of the contributor—it was either a Mrs. A. or a Mrs. B., presumably Ang-los, or the recipe was from Maria, Prudencia, or Angela, who were not dignified by the inclusion of their last names. It is clear that domestic servants were the sources for most of the Mexican recipes. In contrast, Pinedo was from an upper-class family and was aware of a broader range of foodstuffs and culinary preparations from the Mexican tra-dition than that which was presented by the Anglo books.

There is little evidence that Mexican cuisine penetrated Anglo house-holds beyond a few basic recipes. A rare example is the manuscript recipe book of Lillie Hitchcock Coit of San Francisco, written during the 1870s and 1880s.[22] Coit recorded a number of Mexican recipes in the book, which she presumably kept for her country house. These in-cluded a chile sauce from a "Mrs. Sanchez," two *casuelo,* which were chicken stews, a "Mole (Moo-li)" attributed to "William," a chicken in (red) chile, another *mole* with the Frenchified name "Le Mo-le," a chile con carne, and recipes for "Frijoles-Boiled" and "Frijoles-Fried." She also recorded that a good source for Mexican food supplies was the store of José Alcayaga at 524 Broadway. It should be noted that Mrs. Coit was a self-identified gastronome and was probably more adventuresome than others of her class.

Clayton's Quaker Cook Book, published in 1883, was written by H. J. Clayton, who was a professional chef involved in the manufacture of commercial coffee urns. His book is the first one printed that specifically calls for California ingredients, such as an oyster soup using both Eastern and California oysters, chickens from Petaluma, and a "Roman Punch," which includes a pint of California champagne and two gills of good California brandy. However, he provided only two "Spanish" recipes, "Clayton's Spanish Omelette," filled with a mixture of bacon, tomato, mushrooms, and onion, and "Squash and Corn—Spanish Style," which reads as follows:

> Take three small summer squash and three ears of corn; chop the squashes and cut the corn from the cobs. Put into a saucepan a spoonful of lard or butter, and when very hot an onion; fry a little, add the corn and squash, 1 tomato and 1 green pepper, cut small, and salt to taste. Cover closely and stir frequently to prevent scorching.[23]

Another early book is Mary Smith's *Temperance Cook Book*, published in San Jose in 1887. A substantial work of 261 pages, it was written with recipes such that "there should be nothing in our eatables to awaken the appetite of the reformed, and we certainly want nothing to cultivate a taste for intoxicating drinks in the young." The book contains two recipes of Hispanic origin, one for "Spanish Buns—Nice with Coffee" and one for "Chili Colorad" [sic], as follows:

> Take two chickens; cut up as if to stew, when pretty well done, add a little green parsley and two onions. Take half a pound of pepper pods, remove the seeds, and pour on boiling water; steam for ten minutes; pour off the water and rub them in a sieve until all the juice is out; add the juice to the chicken; let it cook for half an hour; add a little butter, flour and salt. Place a border of rice around the dish before setting on the table. This dish may also be made of beef, pork or mutton;

it is to be eaten in cold weather, and is a favorite dish with all people on the Pacific Coast.[24]

The surprising comment about its widespread popularity is unusual, given the general exclusion of Mexican dishes in this and other books of the time, as well as the anti-Mexican food press.

But a number of the books from this period include a section of "Spanish recipes." Typically, these are limited to the most basic recipes. For example, *Treasures Old and New,* by Five Earnest Workers (Los Angeles, 1898), has the following recipes: "Spanish Rice," "Tamales for 150 People," "Mexican Hot Stew," and "Enchiladas."

In 1895 Mary Johnston printed a small pamphlet in Los Angeles called *Spanish Cooking,* which went through three editions and featured recipes for chile sauce, "Albondigas de Callinas" [sic], "Massa" [sic], "Arroze con Tomate," "Colache," and "Panoche."

Charles Lummis became one of the great proselytizers of Hispanic cookery. His *The Landmarks Club Cookbook* was published in 1903, and in it Lummis provided a number of Hispanic recipes from California, Mexico, and South America. Lummis had been responsible for the development of the California fantasy heritage and realized that much of the real heritage had been lost.[25] "The noble old ranches, the noble old Spanish families, are all 'gringoized.' They have Japanese cooks!"[26]

At the beginning of the twentieth century American trade publications began appearing that focused entirely on Mexican cooking, although they were written by Anglos. The first was Harriet Loury's *Fifty Choice Recipes for Spanish and Mexican Dishes,* published in Denver in 1905. May Southworth published *101 Mexican Dishes* in San Francisco the following year, part of a series called *101 Epicurean Thrills,* which she had begun in 1901. Soon, other substantial works appeared, such as May Middleton's *Recipes from Old Mexico* (San Jose, 1909), Bertha Ginger's *California Mexican-Spanish Cook Book* (Los Angeles, 1914), and Frances Belle's *California Cook Book* (Chicago, 1925). The *Los Angeles Times* published a series of cookbooks based on cooking contests from 1902 to 1917, and these had a significant number of recipes in their "Spanish" sections.

It wasn't until the 1930s that more significant works on Mexican cookery were written by Hispanic women. In 1934 the *Mexican Cookbook*, by Erna Fergusson, appeared, based on the recipes of doña Lola Chavez de Armijo, and in 1938 Ana Bégué de Packman published *Early California Hospitality*, which was based on anonymous traditional recipes. But even since that time, works by Hispanic authors describing Mexican food in California have been relatively scarce. Elena Zelayeta produced several books starting in the 1940s,[27] and Jacqueline Higuera McMahan self-published an excellent series of books in the 1980s and 1990s.[28] These were based on family recipes from a Santa Clara County family ranch. Zarela Martínez's mother, Aida Gabilondo, published *Mexican Family Cooking* in 1986. Victor and Mary Lau Valle's *Recipe of Memory: Five Generations of Mexican Cuisine* was a standout when it was published in 1995, earning nominations for both the James Beard and the International Association of Culinary Professionals cookbook awards.

Other ethnic cuisines were not absent in nineteenth-century California. To the contrary, recipes from a variety of European cuisines showed off the sophisticated, but mild, taste of the settlers. In San Francisco in 1881, Mrs. Abby Fisher's *What Mrs. Fisher Knows about Old Southern Cooking* was published, the first cookbook written by an African American. Early Jewish cookbooks, such as *The Unrivalled Cookbook of Los Angeles* by the Ladies of the Temple Bazaar (1902) and the Council of Jewish Women's *Council Cook Book* (San Francisco, 1908–9), also appeared. A number of cookbooks printed in Chinese and Japanese appeared, such as the *Chinese and English Cook Book (Fa ming chung hsi wen ch'u shu pao chien)* (San Francisco, 1910) and Kakichi Yamada's *The Sense of Cooking* (San Francisco, 1928). However, these two books were bilingual, featuring only Anglo and European recipes, and were intended for use by Asian cooks who were servants in middle-class Anglo homes.

Pinedo as a Cook

Pinedo filled her book with a remarkable variety of recipes from the Hispanic, French, and Italian traditions, as well as recipes of her own invention. From the recipes in the book, it is clear that Pinedo was a sophisticated and knowledgeable cook, comfortable in many styles. For example, she provides ten recipes for *adobos* (marinades) and thirteen recipes for *albóndigas* (meatballs). For example, she gives recipes for meatballs done Spanish-style, with veal and chicken (see page 94); delicate ones made with chicken breasts (page 81); German-style, with veal and pork flavored with nutmeg (page 94); Italian-style, with pork, garlic, clove, and mint cooked in a saffron broth (page 95); Catalan-style, with pork and ham, and garlic, clove, saffron, and cumin (page 95); and dumpling-like Spanish meatballs in the German style, with a mixture of bread crumbs and flour, soaked in milk and bound with eggs, then seasoned with thyme, parsley, nutmeg, and pepper (page 96).

It is clear that Pinedo saw her book as an explicit document of cultural transmission, designed to save her culture for her nieces, who were growing up in an Anglo household. As Charles Camp puts it, "Food is one of the most, if not the single most, visible badges of identity, pushed to the fore by people who believe their culture to be on the wane, their daughters drifting from their heritage, their sons gone uptown."[29] Pinedo understood how to employ the symbolic and cultural dimensions of food.

She lived in a time of technological change in the kitchen and clearly had mastered the new stove.[30] In adapting recipes from Mexican sources, she usually removes the traditional instructions on cooking *a dos fuegos* (literally "between two fires," with coals on top and below the pot) and instead instructs readers to put the dish in the oven. She does leave the *dos fuegos* technique intact in the recipe for *carne asada en la olla de los misioneros* (missionary-style pot roast, page 101), possibly because this reminded her of her childhood days at the mission.[31] She had a sense of "historic cookery," as demonstrated in the beefsteak and barbecue recipes.

She was alert to the potential of labor-saving devices and was particularly enthusiastic about the Enterprise Nixtamal corn mill (see the picture of it in this book's illustration section).[32] In her recipe for *nixtamal* (page 134), she declares the Enterprise superior to the *metate*, the traditional stone grinder used for corn, chiles, and seeds.

Pinedo wrote at a time when it was assumed that cooks knew how to cook, that the instruction "make in the usual manner" would be understood by the reader. Before Fannie Farmer introduced level measurements, exact quantities were rarely given, the assumption being that the cook would know the appropriate quantity from experience. Reading the recipes, the modern cook will easily see how much work was involved in preparing food using these traditional techniques. In many Mexican American households, this work continued for decades, even after labor-saving devices became available. Socorro Delgado describes her mother's daily work in the 1930s:

> My mother was always hardworking, even as a child. She would get up real early in the morning and wash the dishes in a tina [large vat]. They had to draw water from a well because they had no sink. She'd

make little baking powder biscuits from scratch every morning for herself and her brothers, and they would take sandwiches to school. She
made tortillas early in the morning when she was very young also.
She made burritos, and they took them to school for lunch. She made
breakfast. They always had potatoes scrambled with eggs. It took a
lot of time to cook because they made everything from scratch. If they
were going to make a caldo [broth], they had to go and pick the vegetables from the garden, and had to wash everything real well. . . .
They roasted their own coffee beans—I did that, too—in a big pan on
top of the stove until they browned to a certain color and it smelled
very good. They stored the roasted coffee in a can and ground it fresh
whenever they made coffee. They boiled the grounds in water and
then filtered it. My mother and Mamina made such wonderful coffee.

Of course, they had the carne seca [dry meat]. They put it in the oven
to roast it a little bit, soaked it, and then pounded it to make *carne
machaca*. This is what they did in their "spare time." They stored the
meat in their "refrigerator"—a cabinet with screen that they would
put outside in the fresh air. And then they would fry the *machaca* with
potatoes or eggs.[33]

Pinedo's book gives ample coverage of traditional dishes, but often
with unexpected interpretations: there are three types of *chilaquiles*
(page 120), one with dried shrimp; there are fourteen recipes for *chiles
rellenos* (stuffed chiles; page 121), including ones with fillings of chicken,
beef, *picadillo*, pork, shrimp, and cod. She serves the *chiles rellenos* fried
in egg batter or, unusual in today's kitchen, in salads, pickled, and
stuffed with white cabbage.

Fish and seafood recipes appear frequently. Cod was a favorite, for
which she offers ten recipes, based primarily on the Iberian tradition,
with Basque and Spanish versions, but also prepared with green chile
and tomato or in a tomato juice flavored with onions, garlic, chiles,
parsley, and oregano.

Her salsas would draw anyone to her table. She gives recipes for fifty-seven varieties (preceding H. J. Heinz by a few years). She prepares nut sauces, mushroom sauces, sauces for meats, oysters, and salads. There is a creole sauce of tomatoes, butter, olives, mushrooms, parsley, oregano, and brown sugar, as well as a hot sauce of red chile and a green-chile sauce. Note that she does not refer to them as *sarsa* or *sarza,* common Californio expressions for salsa.[34]

As is typical of the recipe books of the time, Pinedo presents an extensive selection of preserves, jams, marmalades, and syrups. She includes recipes for preserves of quince (page 169), pears with apples (page 180), figs (page 168), blackberries with strawberries (page 180), pears with figs (page 181), and even tomatoes (page 181). In her introduction, she proscribes beet sugar. This is probably because the first successful beet-sugar factory in the United States was established in Alvarado in 1879, about twenty miles from Santa Clara,[35] and undoubtedly she had an opportunity to sample the product and found it wanting in comparison to cane sugar. The second U.S. beet-sugar factory opened not far away, in Watsonsville in 1887, where Claus Spreckels started the Western Sugar Company. There were problems with the quality control of beet sugar, which often had an unpleasant smell.[36] Beet sugar did not have the same consistent quality as cane sugar until the 1930s.[37]

Pinedo offers both savory and sweet pastries. A corn pudding casserole (page 135) named after her niece Carmencita starts with a dough of freshly grated corn blended with egg yolks, butter, and minced basil. This is covered with a layer of chopped poached beef and pork, then another of chopped onions, hard-cooked eggs, olives, raisins, chopped oregano, cumin, and basil. Over this goes a layer of shredded chicken, more layers of beef and a *picadillo,* a chile sauce, and then a layer of the corn dough. This complex and delicious recipe is clearly an antecedent of the subsequently popularized tamale pie.

There are so many puddings named after her nieces (her sister provided her with eight nieces and three nephews), it's obvious they were a favorite family dish. There are a number of rice puddings, fruit puddings made with lemons or oranges, apples, pineapples, and almonds, and, for her sister, a succulent English bread pudding layered with peaches (page 189).

Encarnación's food was the food of Mexico, brought to California by early settlers and maintained by subsequent contact with central Mexico, through either personal connections or literary transmission. Her food is not the cuisine known today as Cal-Mex, Tex-Mex, and so on, which is Mexican-style food brought to the United States and adapted to American tastes in the various states.

While her cuisine is more directly Mexican, it adapted well to local ingredients. As California became "American" in the period from the 1850s to the 1890s, additional ingredients from the Anglo kitchen became available. The sophisticated food markets of San Francisco were also within easy reach, which may be why she suggests French olives instead of those from California.

She calls for a number of ingredients not commonly available today. *Acitrón* (also known as *cubiertos de biznaga*) is the candied fruit of the barrel cactus, *Echinocactus grandis*. To prepare this, a barrel cactus is harvested and skinned, and the spines removed. Then the pieces are soaked in a brine solution until firm. After this, they are boiled with sugar until crystallized.[38] It is not citron, but that would make a plausible substitution.[39]

Pinedo was not a professional writer, and she took her recipes from multiple sources. Often they seem to be an aide-memoire, but this was the nature of recipe writing at the time. In other recipes, there is a great deal of detail. It seems that she worked from a manuscript compiled over a long period of time. This would have been a family recipe compilation that included traditional Mexican cooking techniques, as well as more modern recipes she collected along the way.

The recipes clearly come from many sources, as they are inconsistent. There are a number of styles used in the recipes, indicating that the collection accreted over time. The duplication of the unusual word *triturate* in two recipes (*crema de vino*, page 170, and *crema de almendras*, page 169) is a clear indication that some recipes shared a common source. Sometimes ingredients are left out—for example, there is no pineapple in the pineapple-orange sherbet (page 170).

In her book Pinedo printed a number of recipes taken from the *Nuevo cocinero mexicano*, which was published in Paris in several editions starting in 1858, including one in 1888, which is probably what she used. Between 15 and 17 percent of her recipes were taken directly from this book. However, she did make sensible adaptations in many of them. She changed the orthography of some words, such as rendering *xitomate* as *tomate*, and shortened cooking times for seafood and vegetables. She also adapted them to the modern stove.

Her book was one of the most complete and balanced that had been published in California. Unlike the Anglo books, which focused on baking, she had recipes for all types of food. For the time, and especially for Mexican cooking, she had a remarkable array of vegetable recipes. At the same time, she had very few dishes that one would class as *sopas secas*, "dry soup" pasta dishes normally served at the beginning of *comidas* (meals).

She had a wide knowledge of the historical literature of cookery. In her introduction, she derides English cookery but makes allusions to a number of early English cookery books. She cites Pegge's *The Forme of Cury*, actually a 1780 edition of Richard II's fourteenth-century recipe book, and Sir Thomas Elyot's (not Elliott) sixteenth-century *The Castel of Helthe*, citing a very rare edition of this early dietary work. She mentions a work by Abraham Veale that is not a cookery book or by Veale (Veale was actually the publisher), A *Direction for the Health of Magistrates and Studentes,* by Gulielmus Gratarolus. She also (mis)cites *Widdovves Treasure* by John Partridge from 1625. Knowing of the existence of these scarce volumes speaks strongly about her education, although her very curious selection of titles and the mistaken details indicate she probably had no personal exposure to them. These books are very rare, and at that time little had been written about culinary history that would have referred to them. Adding to the eccentricity of her list, she fails to mention the best known of the books of early English cookery, such as *The Boke of Kervynge* (1508), *The English Hus-Wife,* by Gervase Markham (1615), or *The Closet of the Learned Sir Kenelm Digby Opened,* by Kenelm Digby (1669).

Encarnación's legacy, *El cocinero español,* was a major culinary production, clear evidence that the Hispanic community harbored cooks of great sophistication who made dishes that showcased a wealth of flavors beyond the ordinary as well as the standard Mexican dishes generally known today. With dishes like these in the Mexican repertoire, it is unfortunate that the cultural segregation extant in California did not allow for a wider appreciation of this cuisine.

Notes

1. There are copies of the book at Arizona State University; the Huntington Library in San Marino, California; Los Angeles Public Library; San Jose Public Library; the University of Santa Clara Library; the University of California at Los Angeles; and the Library of Congress.
2. Clyde Arbuckle, *Santa Clara County Ranchos* (San Jose: Rosicrucian Press, 1973), p. 33.
3. Mrs. Fremont Older [Clara Baggerly], "Relics of a Haunted House," *San Jose News,* May 1, 1926. The shipwreck seems to have been a family legend; apparently there

is no recorded shipwreck that matches this story. He may have been a survivor of the *Natalia*, which sank in Monterey Bay on December 21, 1834. When it sank, most of the passengers were ashore, attending a fiesta (Don B. Marshall, *California Shipwrecks: Footsteps in the Sea* [Seattle: Superior Publishing Company, 1978], p. 43; James A. Gibbs, *Shipwrecks of the Pacific Coast* [Portland, Oreg.: Binfords and Mort, 1962], p. 258). However, the great-grandchildren of Dolores were still telling the story in 2000 (Lorie Garcia, email to author, July 2001).

4. Older, "Relics of a Haunted House."
5. Ibid.
6. Estate of Lorenzo Pinedo, Pinedo will, San Jose County Probate record 74–16838, History San José.
7. Bob Aldrich, "The Old Mill Stream," *Los Gatos Weekly-Times*, March 27, 1996.
8. Julia Tuñón Pablos, *Women in Mexico: A Past Revealed* (Austin: Institute of Latin American Studies, University of Texas Press, 1999), p. 59; quote in Older, "Relics of a Haunted House."
9. C. L. Baldwin, "The Peace Keepers," *Santa Clara Forecast*, January 1993.
10. Mrs. Fremont Older [Clara Baggerly], "William Fitts' Omnibus," *San Jose Mercury*, ca. 1925.
11. Baldwin, "The Peace Keepers."
12. Charles S. McCaleb, *Tracks, Tires, Wires: Public Transportation in California's Santa Clara Valley*, Interurbans Special 78 (Glendale, Calif.: Interurban Press, 1981), p. 5.
13. John C. Super, "Libros de cocina y cultura en América latina temprana," in *Conquista y comida: Consecuencias del encuentro de dos mundos*, ed. Janet Long (Mexico City: Universidad Nacional Autónoma de México, 1996), p. 462.
14. Ibid.
15. Ibid.
16. Josefina Muriel and Guadalupe Pérez San Vicente, "Los hallazgos gastronomicos: Bibliografía de cocina en la Nueva España y el México del siglo XIX," in *Conquista y comida*, ed. Janet Long, p. 469.
17. For example, *Recetario de doña Dominga de Guzman, siglo XVIII* (San Ángel, Mexico: Sanborn's, 1996); *Libro de cocina de D. José Moreda, año 1832* (Oaxaca, Mexico: Circulo Mexicano de Art Culinario, 1987); and the *Colección recetarios antiguos* (Mexico City: Conaculta, 1999–).
18. Sor Juana Inés de la Cruz, *Libro de cocina del Convento de San Jerónimo: Selección y transcripción atribuidas a Sor Juana Inés de la Cruz* (1979; reprint, Toluca, Mexico: Instituto Mexiquense de Cultura, 1996); Muriel and Pérez San Vicente, "Los hallazgos gastronomicos," p. 469.
19. Muriel and Pérez San Vicente, "Los hallazgos gastronomicos," p. 469.

20. Ibid., p. 472. I have not located a copy of this book, and it is absent from Eleanor Lowenstein (*Bibliography of American Cookery Books, 1742–1860* [New York: American Antiquarian Society, 1972]), as well as Jeffrey Pilcher's dissertation appendix, "Cookbooks Printed in Mexico." This lack of U.S. copies indicates it was done for the Mexican market.

21. William Woys Weaver, "Additions and Corrections to Lowenstein's *Bibliography of American Cookery Books, 1742–1860*," *Proceeding of the American Antiquarian Society* 92 (1982): 369. Weaver speculates that the book (Lowenstein, p. 365) was jobbed in Philadelphia because it had the best stereotyping facilities at that time. The actual publisher, the Compañía Estereotipográpfica de la América del Norte, was located in New York.

22. Lillie Hitchcock Coit, *The Recipe Book of Lillie Hitchcock Coit* (Berkeley, Calif.: Friends of the Bancroft Library, 1998).

23. H. J. Clayton, *Clayton's Quaker Cook Book* (San Francisco: Women's Co-operative Printing House, 1883), p. 68.

24. Mary G. Smith, *Temperance Cook Book: For the Benefit of All Housekeepers* (San Jose: Mercury Book and Job Printing House, 1887), p. 64.

25. The fantasy heritage, as described by Carey McWilliams in *North from Mexico: The Spanish-Speaking People of the United States* (New York: Greenwood Press, 1968), pp. 35–47, imagined an early bucolic Spanish California that never existed but was created by California boosters early in the twentieth century.

26. Charles Lummis, *Flowers of Our Lost Romance* (Boston: Houghton Mifflin Company, 1929), p. 273.

27. Elena Zelayeta was a blind restaurateur in San Francisco. Her friends prepared her extremely popular books, which included *Elena's Famous Mexican and Spanish Recipes* (1944), *Elena's Lessons in Living* (1947), *Elena's Fiesta Recipes* (1952), and *Elena's Favorite Foods, California Style* (1967).

28. Jacqueline Higuera McMahan, *California Rancho Cooking* (1983), *The Salsa Book* (1986), *The Red and Green Chile Book* (1988), *The Healthy Fiesta* (1990), *The Mexican Breakfast Book* (1992), *The Chipotle Chile Cookbook* (1994), and *The Healthy Mexican Cook Book* (1994).

29. Charles Camp, *American Foodways: What, When, Why, and How We Eat in America* (Little Rock, Ark.: August House, 1989), p. 29.

30. See Jacqueline B. Williams, *The Way We Ate: Pacific Northwest Cooking, 1843–1900* (Pullman: Washington State University Press, 1996), pp. 39–57, "We Have a Cook Stove," for information on the introduction of the cast-iron stove to the Northwest.

31. Encarnación Pinedo, "Early Days in Santa Clara," *Santa Clara Sunday Bulletin*, June 9, 1901.

32. The Enterprise Manufacturing Company of Philadelphia was established in 1864 and made many kitchen appliances, such as food and coffee grinders, meat choppers, and irons (Ralph Kovel and Terry Kovel, "Discoveries, Collectibles: Bean There, Done That, So Let's Put a Cork in It," *Los Angeles Times*, November 14, 1998). They also published a cookbook with recipes to promote the use of their appliances, *The Enterprising Housekeeper* (editions in 1896, 1898, 1900, 1902).

33. Quoted in Patricia Preciado Martin, *Songs My Mother Sang to Me: An Oral History of Mexican American Women* (Tucson: University of Arizona Press, 1992), p. 59.

34. McMahan, *Rancho Cooking*, p. 45.

35. Fred G. Taylor, *A Saga of Sugar: Being a Story of the Romance and Development of Beet Sugar in the Rocky Mountain West* (Salt Lake City: Utah-Idaho Sugar Company, 1944), p. 69.

36. W. R. Aykroyd, *The Story of Sugar* (Chicago: Quadrangle Books, 1967), p. 110.

37. R. A. McGinnis, *Beet-Sugar Technology*, 2d ed. (Fort Collins, Colo.: Beet Sugar Development Foundation, 1971), p. 509.

38. Preciado Martin, *Songs My Mother Sang*, p. 12.

39. Alan Davidson, *Oxford Companion to Food* (Oxford: Oxford University Press, 1999), p. 3.

The Pinedo residence,
the first house in Santa Clara.
—

Dolores Pinedo and William Fitts.
These photographs were taken at the Clayton
Gallery, at the corner of Santa Clara and
Market Streets, San Jose, about 1878.

———

A sampler that Encarnación Pinedo
made at the age of fourteen.

—

An omnibus on the Alameda between
San Jose and Santa Clara. This is the type of
transportation that William Fitts operated
between Santa Clara and San Jose.

———

Mission Santa Clara, before 1858.
This is where Encarnación Pinedo's parents
and grandparents were married.

—

Ravento and Withrow Market, Santa Clara, about
1900, a market probably similar to one where Pinedo
may have shopped. Note the selection of Christmas
geese hanging throughout the store.
—

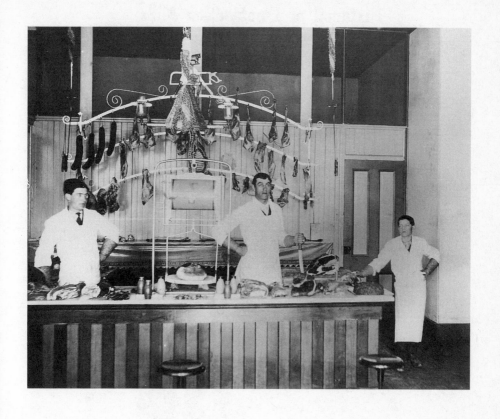

The George Bulmore Market
in east San Jose, about 1903, a typical
meat market of the period.

———

"ENTERPRISE"
Nixtamal or Combination Mills

NIXTAMAL is a corn food product largely used in Mexico, and this mill was primarily designed for grinding the corn so used.

Our development has shown many other purposes where the mill can be used with great advantage, such as grinding cereals, cocoa beans, vanilla beans, poppy seed, peanuts (for peanut butter), white lead, massage cream ingredients and for reducing other materials to pasty substances.

Very adaptable for druggists' use in grinding rosin, ginseng root, herbs, dried berries, pumice stone, coal, etc.

This Nixtamal Mill has the advantage that the cylinder is octagon, which permits the inside screw to get hold of the corn in a most effective way. Of the two knives which make up the mill, one is fastened to the machine by three screws. When the two knives are worn out they can easily be renewed, which makes the machine practically as good as new.

All parts are double tinned, which prevents the "masa" from becoming discolored and also prevents the machine from rusting. The hopper or receptacle is of cast iron, made in one single piece, which permits the operator to exert a pressure on the corn with the free hand.

HAND MILLS AS ABOVE ILLUSTRATED   Prices

No. 54, Weight, 6 pounds; Capacity, 2 pounds per minute, $1.75

No. 64, Weight, 12 pounds; Capacity, 3 pounds per minute, 3.50

Packed 6 in a case

No. 74, Weight, 24 pounds; Capacity, 5 pounds per minute, 7.50

Packed 1 in a case

We can supply an extra hopper (as per illustration) with each hand mill. This hopper will be found very convenient when a large quantity of material is to be ground, as it will allow continuous feeding.

	No. 54	No. 64	No. 74
Prices, each	$ .50	$ .75	$1.50

No. 84, $50.00

Weight, 65½ lbs.; with extra grinders, 73 lbs.

Height, 24 inches.

Length, 12 inches.

Pulley, 12 x 2¾ inches.

Speed of Pulley, 300 revolutions per minute.

Power required, 2 to 3 H. P.

CAPACITY PER HOUR

Corn	4 bushels
Wheat	10 bushels
Oats	10 bushels
Peanuts	250 pounds

Packed in 2 cases

The Enterprise Nixtamal Mill. Pinedo felt the Enterprise was superior to other brands, and a major improvement over the *metate*.

———

TRANSLATOR'S COLLECTION

THE SPANISH COOK

A WORK CONTAINING A THOUSAND VALUABLE AND USEFUL RECIPES TO COOK WITH EASE IN DIFFERENT STYLES

—

Including Advice and Explanations That Put the
Art of Cooking within Reach of Everyone

A NOTE ON THE TEXT

While in her title Encarnación claims over 1,000 recipes, there were actually about 880 in her book. To make the selection for inclusion in this translation, I divided the recipes by subject and then made a proportional selection from each subject. Recipes from the Hispanic tradition were favored over European ones. I included all of the corn-based recipes, such as tamales and enchiladas. Many recipes were redundant—see the recipes for *estofado a la española* for an example—and I generally excluded these from the selection.

Pinedo's original text was arranged alphabetically, probably following the order of the *Nuevo cocinero mexicano,* from which she took so many recipes. To assist the reader, the text has been rearranged in a modern format, grouping recipes by subject, and then roughly alphabetically, which makes it easier to get a sense of the range of Pinedo's accomplishments.

A glossary of unfamiliar foods and techniques is at the end of the book.

Dan Strehl

DEDICATION

To my dear nieces: Mrs. George W. Pollard and Misses Ida Fitts, Angelina Fitts, Erminia Fitts, Leticia Fitts, and Carmencita Fitts.

So that you may always remember the value of a woman's work, study the contents of this volume and take advantage of my knowledge of this art, so important in the management of a family's home. You should consider your needs, because if a woman is rich, she needs to manage; and if she is poor, she needs to know how to work. I have always yearned for your comfort, and many hours of work have been dedicated to compiling, correcting, and writing down the valuable recipes contained in this book, so keep these words as a memory from my heart.

Now, therefore, I dedicate this work to each and every one of you so it will always be there when you know you want your dear aunt.

Encarnación Pinedo
San Jose, July 1898

INTRODUCTION

—

The Art of Cooking

This is one of the arts that very few of those who are called chefs possess in perfection: and even though it is considered one of the most essential accomplishments, its study seems to have been ignored among families in these modern times. In earlier times, the people of the Middle Ages had more or less mastered it, always in accordance with the wealth, opulence, potential, and social position of each nation and its people.

The Persians, said Herodotus, had the custom of celebrating their birthdays, and it was only then that they had great feasts and sacrificed one of their most valued domestic animals to their gods: they roasted it in a barbecue with the finest spices, and all their people dined.

The Greeks were fine gourmets, even though the foods and soups of the Athenians were ridiculed for their frugality.

Notwithstanding that Athenaeus, Archestratus, and many others wrote books about cooking, those all came to be meaningless, because each tribe had the custom of eating different foods. Fish was the only flesh that was commonly used.

To give an idea of the extravagant manner in which they proclaimed their recipes, Archestratus spoke of a "ray cooked in oil, wine and aromatic herbs, with a little grated cheese. Fish stuffed with little fish balls and fried; cooked in marinade; roasted in fig leaves; refreshed in oil; roasted in ashes"; and so on. Such are the recipes they gave.

The Egyptians had the reputation of being great bread eaters, and although they had the finest flours, they made their dough solely with the fruit of a tree called "lotus" or of spelt, a species of wheat that was dried and beaten.[1]

Fish were salted and dried in the sun. Partridges, ducks, and all kinds of small birds were salted and eaten raw. On the occasion of a festival or other rare event, they assuredly ate roasted or cooked beef.

The Romans had their barley gruels called "pulses," and these were the principal food of the people, together with all kinds of vegetables. Very little meat was used. Lucullus introduced some new ideas in the art of cooking, and Apicius earned a reputation that made him celebrated in this art as it then existed. The Romans almost always prepared and cooked their foods with oil.

The Germans seem to have given little or no importance to the style in which their meals were prepared.

The English have advanced the art a bit, enough that several of its writers have published on the subject: a Mr. Pegge in 1390, Sir J. Elliot in 1539, Abraham Veale in 1575, and Widovas Treasure in 1625.[2] Despite all this, there is not a single Englishman who can cook, as their foods and style of seasoning are the most insipid and tasteless that one can imagine.

The French and Italians have been the most advanced, although the French system was very imperfect until the Italian taste was intro-

---

1. Although described this way by classical authors Theophrastus, Diodorus, and Pliny, "lotus tree" bread was actually made from the aquatic lotus. Spelt was never found in ancient Egypt, and the wheat she refers to was in fact emmer (William J. Darby, *Food: The Gift of Osiris* [New York: Academic Press, 1977], vol. 2, pp. 489, 522, 642).—*Translator*

2. See page 36 for the identification of these titles.—*Translator*

duced in France by the princesses of the royal house of the Medici; since then the excellence of the French makes them the best cooks in the world. They discovered that meats could and ought to be basted with their own juices or broths while they were cooking.

The esteem of a good chef can only be known when we take note of the wages they earn in the opulent homes of affluent families, in first-class hotels, and in clubs of prominent persons in large and populous cities.

The truth is that in our times it is thought that this art is one of the most enviable accomplishments of a woman; and it is now treated as one of the most precious and necessary branches of her education, so much so that in England and in the United States today, schools of cooking have been established, even though without a very happy result; it seems generally that only young women of a humble and poor lineage dedicate themselves to this very important study.

I am quite convinced that the time has come when the knowledge of cooking will be obligatory; and the art will receive a major impetus because the great importance of knowing how to prepare, season, and temper foods for the fire, making them ready to help in the digestion in the human stomach, will become evident; and I have resolved to publish this book, which I have entitled *The Spanish Cook without Equal,* because its like has never been brought to light, so explicit, complete, and compendious, with long explanations and details for cooking in all styles and with the greatest ease.

For the benefit of my subscribers I offer the following advice, which I hope will not seem excessive, when one takes into account that ninety-nine out of one hundred cooks don't know what I am speaking about, but they should know the following.

Kitchen Cleanliness

Cleanliness is undoubtedly the cardinal virtue of every cook.

Foods are much more appetizing and healthy when they are cooked in a clean and tidy manner.

Many lives have been sacrificed because of a lack of cleanliness in bronze, copper, and ceramic pots; the first two types must always be kept lustrous and clean inside and out; they can and should be cleaned on the inside with salt and hot vinegar every time you want to cook something in them, and no greasy or acid substance should be allowed to set in them after it has been cooked.

Everything in the kitchen should be maintained with the greatest cleanliness possible, and leftovers or scraps and the rest of food not used for the preparation of soups should be thrown out the moment it is no longer needed.

The same observations that were made with respect to copper kitchenware and so on are applicable to all utensils and the clothing of a good cook, who should have these fundamental objectives: first, cook all your dishes and soups according to the requirements of the rules of the art; and secondly, be pure and clean, in your person and in your work, for that way you will always merit the praises of your patrons or admirers: then, as we said before, *cleanliness is the cardinal virtue of the cook.*

And now, since cooks need to use some judgment in their work, I do not think it is unreasonable for me to give some advice here, consistent with my extensive experience and study of this enviable art.

We start with the principle that all who sit down at table to eat expect good food; and we cannot pardon mistakes made by the cook, or give excuses when the palate ends up unhappy after having paid good money.

When meat forms the principal part of the meal, one must know if it is of good or bad quality, and this is how:

When the meat from a steer is good, it should be relaxed and red, and the fat yellowish. The meat from a cow, on the contrary, should have a fine grain and be more faded, and the fat should be medium white. Bad meat is obtained from animals badly fed or too old; it can be spotted in the hardness of the fat, blackish and corroded meat, and in the thick nerves across the ribs. When you press a piece of meat and it springs back after you remove your fingers, you can be sure that the animal is good and healthy and in its prime. When you press a piece of meat with your finger, if it does not rise promptly after removing the finger, nor recovering the imprint made by the pressure, the animal was old and maybe ill, or at least of an inferior quality, and you should not use the meat.

The meat from beef is cooked or roasted in the styles indicated by the recipes in this book.

Selecting Ingredients

The Jewish prohibition against the meat of pork, as a dirty food, was based on the intrinsic uncleanness of this animal.

An article appeared in one of the monthly magazines that gave a succinct report of the sickly constitution of the pig. The article said that in Vermont, New Hampshire, Maine, and other eastern states, where the inhabitants must vaccinate their livestock, almost all the pigs sent to the market in Boston, and there are thousands of them, are sick with scrofula, salt phlegm, rashes, herpes, and bad blood humors. These and many other calamities can occur through the use of meat from sick pigs, and the famous Dr. Brainard assured the author that it has been calculated, and with reason, that more than half the pigs in this country are unhealthy. You must use good judgment and care to select a suckling pig or a piece of pork to cook.

The cook should be convinced that the pork was fattened only with grain or clean food, or that the mothers of the suckling pigs were from the farm and were fattened purely with corn and other clean and nutritious grain.

The way to make stews with pork are listed in their appropriate place.

The same rules given above for selecting beef serve for lamb.

To select poultry, watch for the following: if a cock, there should be small, unclipped spurs, and if a hen, it should have smooth crest and feet. When you buy dead ones be careful to smell them carefully, and feel the breast to see if they have meat there. If not, it is probable that they died from illness and shouldn't be eaten.

The way to choose a goose is as follows: If the goose is young, it should have a yellow beak; a red beak is a sign of age. If it is fresh, it should have very flexible feet when dead; if they are rigid, the bird is old and dry.

In selecting fish, of whatever species, only look to see if the eyes are brilliant and the body rigid and very straight; this is an infallible sign that it is fresh.

Select eggs by putting them in a pan of water; if they stay on the bottom, they are good; if they stand on their points, they are bad and should not be eaten.

You can tell when flour is good by taking a fistful in your hand and squeezing it firmly: if it compacts and stays in a mass, it is of the best quality, and the dough you make from it will be smooth, flexible, and elastic. An adulterated flour is much heavier than the better flour, and is hard to compress; if you try it as described above, it will not give the same result.

Second—take a small quantity and rub between your fingers; if it is smooth and flexible, it is good, and if it is sticky and rough, it is bad.

Third—put a little bit on the table and blow softly with your breath; if it leaves little piles on the table that resisted the action of the breath, it is good, and if it completely spreads out, it is bad.

Fourth—put a thimbleful in the palm of your hand and rub smoothly with your finger: if the flour smooths out and stays slippery, it is of an inferior quality; and if, on the contrary, it seems rough in the hand, like fine sand, it is good.

Mushrooms are one of the most dangerous condiments, and the way of knowing for certain is the following: take the mushroom and put salt in the spongy part underneath: if it turns yellow, it is poisonous, but if it turns black, it is good.

Butter is clarified in a hot bath. Allow it to settle and pour off only the clear part, cooling it as soon as possible. Butter clarified in this way will stay good and fresh a long time.

Rancid butter is fixed this way: boil it in water with a little charcoal (let us say a tenth part) to remove the rancidity. Once it is melted, let it rise to the surface and leave it to settle, then take it out carefully with a spoon. It will remain absolutely fresh, but it will lose the flavor of table butter and can only be used in stews in the kitchen.

Select nutmeg by pricking it with a pin: if oil comes out, it is good.

General Principles

It is preferable to use a small pan or an enamel pot to make preserves or jams and good white sugar, but never beet sugar.

The good cook ought to have a supply of various spices. Some dishes, and the most exquisite ones, cannot be made without them. Whole-grain pepper is preferable to ground.

Observations

First—you should never let jams cool in a copper vessel, because of verdigris.

Second—you should examine the papers that cover them from time to time, and change them if they are damaged.

Third—when preserves show the least thing that would make you throw them out, you can boil them for a few minutes, but they lose their flavor.

Fourth—you must keep preserves in a cool place, but sheltered from humidity. Heat starts a fermentation that progresses quickly, and the humidity makes them moldy.

EL COCINERO ESPAÑOL

RECETAS · RECIPES

SOPAS, PAN, HUEVOS

SOUPS, BREADS, EGGS

SOPAS · SOUPS

Albóndigas a la española
SPANISH-STYLE MEATBALL SOUP

Chop pork loin until it is minced or ground, and remove any sinews. Then add finely chopped green onion, peeled and seeded tomatoes, parsley, fresh or dry coriander, and garlic.

Add a piece of cornmeal paste [*nixtamal*] or a spoonful of cornmeal, one or two raw eggs, bread crumbs, a piece of lard or butter, salt, and pepper.

Mix these together by hand, forming meatballs as usual, then add them to the boiling stock. If there is no stock, cook in boiling water.

Season the broth with tomato, green onion, chopped parsley, salt, pepper, and butter. Thicken the broth with beaten egg yolks when ready to serve.

Albóndigas de frailes
FRIARS' MEATBALL SOUP
—

Chop pork, onions, garlic, parsley, mint, thyme, oregano, bread crumbs, and eggs together; add a little butter; mix it all very well and make the meatballs a larger size than usual, then put them in boiling water. Add to the broth a paste made with meat and more butter.

When they are done, thicken the broth with egg yolks and flour dissolved in cold water.

Sopa de frijoles colorados
RED BEAN SOUP
—

Cook the beans in broth with a large piece of ham, a large carrot cut in two, an onion with two whole cloves, and a sprig of parsley and celery.

When done, remove the ham and the vegetables. Mash the beans well, and pass them through a sieve.

Pour the puree in the broth, and bring it to a boil. Serve in a tureen garnished with slices of fried bread or toast, which are added just before serving.

Sopa de queso
CHEESE SOUP
—

Finely chop equal amounts of onions, tomatoes, parsley, and chile.

Fry this mixture in very hot lard, and when it is half done, add some beaten eggs, cheese cut in small cubes, and salt.

Mix and turn, and before the eggs set, pour in some boiling water.

This soup should be served very hot and should have a good consistency.

MENUDO · TRIPE

Menudo o clamole castellano
CASTILIAN TRIPE STEW

Put some calves' feet on to cook with the tripe, all well washed and cut into medium pieces. Let simmer for two or three hours, then flavor with some very ripe tomatoes, chopped onions, garlic, parsley or mint, salt, and pepper. Cover the marmite well to finish cooking [see *marmite* in Ingredients and Procedures section—*Translator*].

This tripe is served very hot with toasted bread.

Menudo a la española
SPANISH-STYLE TRIPE

Cut the tripe in uniform pieces, adding the double tripe. Cut them in strips with a knife, and then cut it in pieces. [Add] two cows' feet divided in pieces, or some calves' feet, [and] a cup of well-washed hominy. After boiling the tripe for three hours, flavor with toasted chile, ground in a mortar with some garlic cloves, chopped onion, mint, and salt.

The tripe should cook for six hours on a slow fire without interruption, with the casserole or pot well covered.

Menudo o clamole de carnero
TRIPE OR LAMB CHILE STEW

Fry soaked ancho chiles ground with cooked tomatoes, cumin, and fried bread in lard; add some thin slices of tongue if you wish. Pour all this on the tripe, which was cut in uniform pieces and cooked in water with salt and its broth. Cook it until well seasoned and until it becomes soupy but not watery. Serve it with toasted bread.

PUCHERO · STEW

Take from two to six pounds of beef, wash it well, and put [it] in a pot of boiling water and salt.

Put it on a moderate fire, and increase the heat from time to time until you have removed the scum and it stops appearing.

Leave the pot for a period of five or six hours over an even and temperate fire, and after the first three have passed, put in two medium-sized carrots, two turnips, a rape, Galician cabbage, a handful of parsley, a roasted onion with two or three cloves, and salt. You can add a whole bird or half a hen, the giblets of a turkey, or the bones of a lamb roast.

This is made in a style so simple and easy, it is the best there is of this type of cooking.

Half a gallon or a quarter gallon of water for a pound of meat.

Puchero de cola de buey
OXTAIL STEW

—

Chop an oxtail in as many pieces as it has vertebrae, and wash it well in fresh water.

Then put it in a pot of boiling water and skim off the foam that rises to the top. When there is no more foam, add a cup of garbanzo beans.

Cover the pot, and let the stew simmer for two hours over a moderate flame. Add a chopped onion, tomato, leek, celery, parsley, salt, and pepper.

Half an hour before serving, add three spoonfuls of well-washed rice.

To make a good oxtail stew requires no less than five hours.

Advice: garbanzos should be put to soak in salted cold water the night before, and on the next day they should be rinsed and put in fresh water until added to the stew.

PANES · BREADS

Acemitas
SEMOLINA ROLLS

—

Add a good piece of raw lard, a teaspoon of salt, and a teaspoon of soda dissolved in a little milk to a quart of flour sifted with two teaspoons of cream of tartar.

Then roll out the dough on the table with a rolling pin. Cut the rolls with a mold or a knife as big as you need. When rolling the dough, make it a quarter inch thick.

Bollos a la inglesa
ENGLISH-STYLE ROLLS

—

Put a half quart of flour in a bowl, and push it up the sides with a spoon. Add half a cup of powdered sugar, one-half teaspoon salt, a tablespoon of butter, and a cup of yeast and another of warm milk. Beat strongly for several minutes. After beating, cover it and put in a warm place. Leave it there all night. The following morning add more flour to make a smooth dough. Cover it again and let it rise. Then put it on the table and roll it with a pin until [it's] an inch thick. Cut the rolls with a pastry cutter, spread the dough with butter, and fold them in half. Put these on tin baking sheets, cover, and put in a sheltered place to rise.

These rolls should be baked in a moderate oven for twenty minutes.

BUÑUELOS · FRITTERS

Buñuelos de Valparaiso
VALPARAISO FRITTERS

———

Make a dough with two egg yolks and half a tablespoon of salt. Make a stiff dough, roll it out with a pin, and cut [it] into small half-inch squares. Fry them in very hot lard.

Add some extract or a glass of sherry or maraschino, cinnamon [see Ingredients and Procedures section—*Translator*], the juice of a lemon to a prepared white-sugar syrup. Place the fritters in a fancy dish with cleaned, toasted walnuts, pour on the syrup, and then serve the fritters.

Buñuelos, o pasta de freir
FRITTERS, OR DOUGH TO FRY

———

Mix enough good flour with water, add a little sugar, a spoonful of oil, and one or two spoonfuls of orange-blossom water.

Immediately mix in egg whites beaten to snowy peaks. Note that the batter must have an adequate consistency to cover the apples or other ingredients with a single dip.

Immerse the fruits or whatever you are making in the batter, and fry in very hot fat. Serve very hot, sprinkled with powdered sugar.

Buñuelos, o suspiros de monjas
PUFFY FRITTERS, OR NUNS' SIGHS

———

Mix about two ounces of butter, salt, and sugar with a half quart of water in a casserole.

Bring it to a boil, stirring constantly with a spoon, adding dry flour until it forms a stiff dough. Remove it from the fire and let it cool. Add six egg yolks, one at a time, beating constantly until they are all incorporated. If the dough is too stiff, add egg yolks and vanilla. Take pieces of the dough and fry them in very hot lard.

Drain them, and serve powdered with sugar.

EMPANADAS · TURNOVERS

Masa para empanadas
TURNOVER DOUGH

———

Add two egg yolks and one white, a small piece of lard, and salt to a pound and a half of flour. Mix it together with cold water, knead it well, and when it reaches the right consistency, form the pastry circles, fill them, and put them in the oven.

Empanadas de calabaza sazonas
SPICED SQUASH TURNOVERS

———

Cook the squash in large pieces, and take it off the fire when done. Mash well, and pass through a sieve, spicing with ground cinnamon, very little clove, and sugar.

Fill the turnovers, fold them over, and seal the edges before baking in the oven.

Empanadas de frijol
BEAN TURNOVERS

—

Cook the beans well, then grind them or pass them through a sieve. Then fry them slowly in butter, adding clear syrup or sugar to taste, and ground cinnamon. Let the flavor develop over low heat. Stuff the pastry circles with the beans, and fry or bake in the oven.

Empanadas de picadillo de carne de buey
SPICED BEEF TURNOVERS

—

Chop a good piece of raw meat, carefully removing the nerves. Fry three or four garlic cloves, and when they begin to color, remove them and add the meat. Let it brown, then add chopped onion, peeled and seeded tomato, olives, raisins, oregano, pepper, and salt.

When you see the picadillo [see Ingredients and Procedures section— Translator] start to dry, add a teaspoon of flour with a little water. Let it thicken, then fill the pastry circles and bake them.

Also, you can add red-chile sauce and fry them or bake in the oven.

∾

Levadura
YEAST

—

Peel three or four regular potatoes, wash them in fresh water, and grate them with a grater. Add three ounces of flour, two of sugar, and one of salt. Beat together with a spoon, then add boiling water, a little at a time, stirring the mixture so that it doesn't solidify.

Let it cool, then incorporate a little piece of prepared yeast that has been dissolved in a little warm water, or a cup of yeast from a previous batch.

Put the yeast mixture in an earthenware crock, and store in a cool place for use when needed.

Take two cups of yeast with the flour you need and beat it vigorously. The yeast should have the consistency of a soft paste. It will rise well when used.

Before finishing the yeast in the crock, you have to make a fresh batch, taking a cup of it and putting it with the potatoes and a square of yeast dissolved in warm water.

With this method, so simple, you have fresh yeast every day.

The yeast in the crock will last eight days.

∾

Pan de maíz
CORNBREAD

Separate the whites and yolks of four or six eggs, and beat them. When the whites are very stiff, add ten ounces of sugar and the beaten yolks.

Add two tablespoons of flour and two tablespoons of cream of tartar or baking powder to the cornmeal. Carefully mix the flours before adding the beaten eggs, two ounces of melted butter, a cup of very rich milk, and a teaspoon of soda dissolved in a little milk.

Beat it and add more flour until the batter is smooth.

Grease a baking dish with lard and pour in the batter. Just before it is completely done, moisten with a well-cooked syrup. Cut the bread before taking it out of the baking dish, and serve it very hot. It can be baked in molds in the oven.

The quantity of eggs and butter vary according to taste.

White corn flour is preferable for bread.

Pan de maíz fresco
FRESH CORNBREAD

—

Grind the corn in a *metate* or grate with a grater. When the corn paste is ready, add a good piece of butter, a cup of fresh milk, a teaspoon of salt, one or two teaspoons of baking powder, and four beaten eggs, separating the whites from the yolks. Beat the yolks with four ounces of granulated sugar and mix with the whites before adding to the corn.

Mix everything well and then pour in a baking dish greased with lard. Cook the bread in a medium oven, and be sure to serve it very hot.

∾

Pasteles o empanadas a la argentina
ARGENTINE-STYLE PASTRIES OR TURNOVERS

—

Make a *picadillo* from raw beef; fry four crushed garlic cloves in lard, and remove them as soon as they begin to take on color.

Then, add the beef, and when it starts to cook, add three chopped onions. Let them cook for a while, and add three or four tomatoes and four seeded and skinned green chiles, all finely chopped, and season with pepper, oregano, cumin, and salt.

Next, separately fry three medium-sliced onions, adding five finely chopped, skinned, and seeded large tomatoes, four of the biggest green chiles, which should be finely chopped without skin or seeds, olives, seedless raisins, powdered oregano, cumin, pepper, and salt, with some olives in oil.

Separately, cook three or four chickens, though not completely. After cooling, cut them in medium pieces and put in the sliced-onion sauce.

Take a tray or a baking dish, spread it thoroughly with lard, and line well with a pastry dough.

Place a good layer of pastry in the bottom of the dish and pour on the *picadillo*, then a layer of chicken sauce, and then another of the *picadillo*.

Then cover the pie with the pastry, baste with syrup, and cook in the oven at a moderate heat.

TORTILLAS

Tortillas de harina a la española
SPANISH-STYLE FLOUR TORTILLAS

—

Put two pounds of sifted flour on a tray with half an ounce of salt, an egg yolk, and a good piece of raw lard.

Moisten the lard with warm milk, mix the ingredients, and knead the dough loosely and firmly for two minutes.

Let the dough rest before making the tortillas. Cook them on a *comal*, and brown them over the coals [see *comal* in Ingredients and Procedures section—*Translator*].

They also can be cooked on the stove.

Tortillas de agua
WATER TORTILLAS

—

Make a dough with two pounds of sifted flour, a half ounce of salt, and an ounce of lard.

Knead with warm water, being careful not to make it tough.

Knead it loosely, leaving it tender. Let it rest for a bit. Form into small balls, and rest on a napkin sprinkled with flour. Then make the tortillas.

HUEVOS · EGGS

Tortilla de huevos
OMELETTE
—

Carefully beat eight or ten fresh eggs without separating the yolks and whites, adding two tablespoons of fresh water. Season with salt, pepper, parsley, and finely chopped green onions. You can also add some artichoke hearts or cooked asparagus, or three tablespoons of grated cheese.

Heat a frying pan and melt a small piece of fresh lard, and put in the beaten eggs, turning them constantly until they begin to set, and when they do, lift them with the point of a knife and put a small piece of fresh lard under them, folding the omelette on top of itself in the style of an empanada.

Place it on a platter, and serve it hot.

Tortilla de huevos con aguardiente
BRANDY OMELETTE
—

Beat eight fresh eggs, separating the yolks and whites. Mix in three tablespoons of powdered sugar with the yolks, [then] beat together with three tablespoons of cream and a little salt added at the last moment.

Mix the whites and the prepared yolks together and whip it all briskly, then fry the omelette in olive oil.

When done, put the omelette in a serving dish and cover it with sugar that you have toasted in an iron skillet.

When everything is ready, cut into squares and sprinkle with a glass of brandy and then set on fire. Serve the omelette as soon as the fire goes out.

Albondiguillas fritas
LITTLE FRIED FORCEMEAT

Cook the eggs and finely chop the whites; mash the yolks well and add chopped parsley and a very thick custard sauce. Mix well, form into balls, roll in bread crumbs, then egg, and fry them.

Serve them sprinkled with parsley.

Huevos hipócritas (con jamón)
HYPOCRITES' EGGS (WITH HAM)

Cut some thin slices of ham, fry them in butter, and when they are done, place them in a plate and pour on the butter in which they were fried. Put the eggs on top of each slice and sprinkle with pepper and nutmeg. Put over a very slow fire to set, and once set, carry them to the table.

Huevos revueltos
SCRAMBLED EGGS

Make a good sauce of onion, tomato, green chiles, oregano, and salt. When it is well seasoned, beat the whites and yolks of some eggs. Mix everything together in the pan and stir slowly with a spoon until the eggs are soft and tenderly set.

Huevos revueltos con longanizas o salchichón
SCRAMBLED EGGS WITH *LONGANIZA* OR SAUSAGE

Fry the *longanizas* [see Ingredients and Procedures section—*Translator*] and break them up in the lard, then remove them and fry chopped onions and tomatoes in the same lard.

Beat the whites and yolks of several eggs, separating some from the others. Mix everything together in a frying pan and stir a little at a time until the egg is tenderly set.

PESCADO

FISH

Albondiguillas de merluza
HAKE FISHBALLS

—

Cook the hake in salted water; remove the bones and the skin, keeping only the meat, and chop it finely. Beat a portion of the hake with eggs (whites and yolks), fried chopped onion, parsley, salt, peppers, raisins, or sugar to smooth the dish. Mix everything together and make fishballs from the paste. Fry them in lard or olive oil, keeping the fishballs apart with a spoon.

Make a sauce in the same frying pan in which the fishballs were cooked. To do this, sprinkle a little flour over the cooking residue; add a few drops of vinegar and finely chopped parsley. Add some boiling water to the sauce, and add the fishballs.

BACALAO · COD

Bacalao en aceite y tomate
SALT COD IN OIL AND TOMATO

—

Soak the cod for twenty-four hours, then bring it to a simmer in a little water. Remove it and break into small pieces.

Fry the cod in a casserole with a little olive oil, some sliced onion, chopped parsley, seeded and peeled tomato, and some quartered chiles.

After everything has fried in the oil, add the broth the cod was cooked in, salt, and pepper as needed. Simmer over a low flame.

Bacalao a la española
SPANISH-STYLE SALT COD

—

Soak a good piece of cod in fresh water overnight to remove the salt. The next day, rinse it several times and cook it.

When done, drain it and remove the bones and skin. Shred it with your hands and remove any bones.

Mix the cod pieces with some beaten eggs and make large, thick cakes. Fry in very hot lard.

Place the cod cakes in a tomato or red-chile sauce and let them simmer about ten minutes over very low heat.

Bacalao en tomate y chile verde
SALT COD IN TOMATO AND GREEN CHILE

—

After cooking the cod, separate into slices and remove the bones, being careful not to make the pieces too small.

Fry onion in lard with a nice red tomato, a clove or two of garlic, and chopped green chile. The fried mixture should cover the fish. Put layers of the fried mixture and the fish in a casserole, adding some bread crumbs moistened with vinegar to thicken the sauce.

Cover the casserole, simmer *a dos fuegos* slowly, for more than half an hour, without touching it, until ready to be served [see Ingredients and Procedures section—*Translator*].

Bacalao en salsa de chile
SALT COD IN CHILE SAUCE

—

Soak the cod the night before; devein a little chile and the next day grind it [together] with garlic. Fry the chile in oil with toasted bread.

Add water to the chile and then add the raw cod, cut into small pieces, with olives, chopped parsley, and oregano.

Bacalao con pan rallado y queso
SALT COD WITH BREAD CRUMBS AND CHEESE

—

Fry very well in olive oil [some] onion, chopped parsley, two roasted and ground tomatoes, some grated bread crumbs, pepper, and oregano.

Add the fish after having soaked out the salt. Use large pieces with oil, small chiles, and olives.

Add the cheese when the cod is served.

Bacalao a la bizcáina
BASQUE-STYLE SALT COD

—

Desalt the cod overnight in fresh water. The next day, rinse it several times. Drain it well, remove the bones and skin, and cut it into small pieces. Put a casserole on the fire with four or five tablespoons of olive oil, [add] four finely chopped garlic cloves, and fry them until golden.

Then add two or three chopped onions [and] potatoes cut in squares and fried, together with the cod. Let it all fry; add six or eight seeded and peeled tomatoes, parsley, olives, oregano, and pepper. Cover the casserole closely, and put it at the back of the stove so it can cook on a slow fire for a long time.

Bacalao con queso
SALT COD WITH CHEESE

—

After removing the salt and cooking the cod, shred it and remove the bones. Add grated cheese, cover with bread crumbs and a little cream and butter, and put in the oven.

Bacalao en salsa blanca
SALT COD IN WHITE SAUCE

—

Let the cod desalt for a night. The following day, rinse several times before putting it on to cook.

When finished, take it out of the water. Carefully remove the skin and bones; finally, shred it a little and put [it] into a white sauce.

OSTRAS · OYSTERS

Open a dozen oysters, carefully collecting the fluid they contain and passing it through a sieve. Warm this without boiling and put the oysters in for a few minutes. Drain them and place in a dish with a good piece of butter, shallots, parsley, [and] chives, all chopped very fine, and a spoonful of olive oil, pepper, and grated nutmeg. Cover them well with a layer of grated bread and put the platter in the oven. When the bread crumbs take some color, remove from the oven and sprinkle with lemon juice.

Ostras a la española
SPANISH-STYLE OYSTERS
———

Desalt and then cook the oysters. Take some onion, a little garlic, and parsley, and put them on the fire in a casserole with lard, so they only steep without boiling or browning.

Drain the oysters, keeping a little of the broth in which they cooked. Thicken the broth with ground, dry toast crumbs.

Season with pepper, adding a little olive oil.

Ostras fritas en aceite
OYSTERS FRIED IN OIL
—

To begin, remove the oysters from the shell, put them together in a napkin, keeping them moist, and sprinkle lightly with salt.

Beat two eggs, whites and yolks, and add two tablespoons of olive oil or lukewarm melted lard.

First dredge the oysters in bread crumbs, then in the egg, and then again in the bread. After breading, fry them in olive oil or lard, which should be very hot.

Fry the oysters two or three minutes, until well browned. Drain them and put on the serving platter. This is dressed with watercress or parsley.

Use a wooden spoon and a fork to lift the oysters.

PESCADO · FISH

Pescado relleno
STUFFED FISH
—

Gut and clean a good sturgeon, filling with fish stuffing. Sprinkle with salt and pepper.

Grease a large heavy paper with lard, covering it with parsley, tarragon, and green garlic. Put the stuffed sturgeon on top, larded with anchovies.

Roll up the paper, wrapping in the sturgeon, which is put to cook slowly on the grill, sprinkling frequently.

The roast sturgeon is served with a white sauce of anchovies and capers.

Pescado en estofado
BRAISED FISH

Prepare one or two carp, cut in pieces. Fry a dozen spring onions in fresh lard without letting them take on too much color, then add a spoonful of flour. Let this fry a bit, then add half a bottle of white wine, a cup of hot water, a handful of mushrooms, a bay leaf, parsley, pepper, salt, and chopped fresh garlic. Put the fish in the casserole and simmer over a moderate fire.

Just before serving, bind the sauce with three egg yolks after removing the casserole from the fire. Put the fish on the platter and add some slices of fried bread.

Pescado asado a la parilla
GRILLED FISH

Marinate a shad in fine oil for an hour with finely chopped parsley, basil, tarragon, shallot, salt, and pepper, turning the fish in the marinade. Cook the shad on the grill over a slow fire, turning it once or twice, sprinkling it with the oil from the marinade.

Serve with a spicy sauce.

Pescados blancos rellenos de avellanas y almendras
WHITEFISH STUFFED WITH HAZELNUTS AND ALMONDS

—

Toast the hazelnuts and almonds, then grind them.

Fry them in butter, sprinkling with cinnamon, and use this to stuff the gutted and cleaned whitefish. Coat with grated bread, pepper, and salt, and wrap in greased paper. Put on the grill or fry in lard, taking care to turn them so they cook evenly on both sides.

If they're fried, there is no need to wrap in paper.

To serve them, sprinkle with vinegar or lemon.

Pescado en aceite y vino
FISH IN OIL AND WINE

—

Fry onions, a little garlic, [and] parsley, all chopped in a little oil. Add a little water and the fish, and let cook over a mild fire.

Add olive oil and a little white wine, in the proportion of a half quart of each for three fish.

Add a slice of toasted bread, grated for thickening, and some olives and rosemary.

Pescado en aceite
FISH IN OIL

—

Grease a casserole with lard and put some oil in it. If the barbel are not fresh, desalt them, and slice them.[1]

Fry some deveined ancho chile in lard, and when well done, grind it.

Put a layer of the fish in the casserole, and sprinkle with pepper, Italian oregano, olives, and grated toasted bread.

Put on another layer of the fish covered the same way, repeating this until the casserole is full.

Truchas rellenas y empapeladas
STUFFED TROUT WRAPPED IN PAPER

—

After cleaning and scaling the trout, stuff them with ground almonds, olives, ground peppers, chiles, onions, and chopped parsley, seasoned with salt, pepper, oregano, capers, oil, and vinegar.

When stuffed, cover them with grated bread crumbs, salt, and pepper, sprinkle with olive oil, and wrap in paper spread with lard.

Put them on the grill to roast, turning them carefully.

They also can be fried in lard or baked in butter without wrapping them in paper.

1. The recipe calls for barbel (*bobo*), a fish from the tidewaters of Veracruz. It is eaten fresh along the coast but salted for sale in the interior of Mexico. It was probably not available in California.—*Translator*

Pescado asado ahumado con laurel
GRILLED FISH SMOKED WITH BAY LEAVES

———

After cleaning the fish, wipe it dry and spread with a mixture of salt, pepper, lemon juice, and olive oil.

Put in on the grill, and place some bay leaves on the coals under it from time to time so the fish receives all the smoke.

Turn the fish frequently, basting it with the above ingredients until golden.

Serve with finely chopped green onions and parsley.

Pescado salmón asado a la parilla
GRILLED SALMON

———

Marinate some good pieces of salmon in olive oil, turning them in the oil, and sprinkle with salt and pepper.

Wrap each piece in thick paper greased with oil and cook on the grill on a very moderate fire.

When the salmon is grilled properly, remove the paper and serve with some sauces.

AVES

—

POULTRY

Albóndigas delicadas
DELICATE FORCEMEAT

—

Cut raw poultry breasts into small pieces, simmer them, then grind or chop them until they are reduced to a paste.

Take a good piece of white bread that has been fried [and] then simmered in broth, and put it in the mortar with the poultry breasts, and add pepper, salt, nutmeg, a piece of butter the size of an egg, very finely chopped green onions, two shallots, and some cooked egg yolk.

Mix all together and form the meatballs with your hands, then put them in the broth to cook.

∾

Aves en pipián de ajonjoli
FOWL IN SESAME SAUCE

—

After roasting or cooking some tomatoes, squeeze out the seeds; devein and brown some ancho chiles in lard, ten per eight tomatoes, then grind them with a cup of toasted sesame seeds or peanuts.

Start frying everything in lard, and add ten skinned walnuts, finely ground with some pine nuts. When done, add some water, and pour everything into the pot you are going to stew the birds in, along with a little whole sesame, *acitrón*, pepper, *tornachiles*, cinnamon, vinegar, and salt [for *acitrón* and *tornachile*, see Ingredients and Procedures section— *Translator*]. Add the salt last so the sauce doesn't thicken.

Asadas en pipián de pepitas de melon y almendras
ROAST BIRDS IN MELON SEED AND ALMOND SAUCE

Devein red chiles and toast them well in lard; likewise toast a piece of bread and then grind them together. Then separately grind a handful of cleaned and toasted almonds and another of melon seeds, and then put them in water to cook.

After frying the chile and the ground bread, add the broth of almonds and melon seeds. Simmer until it's thickened, season with salt, remove from the fire, and bathe the roast birds in the *pipián*.

Aves en mole gallego
BIRDS IN GALICIAN SAUCE

Devein pasilla chile and toast in lard, then grind with cinnamon, cloves, a handful of pine nuts, another of cleaned walnuts, another of toasted sesame seeds, and lots of almonds: fry everything in very hot lard, then add the hen or turkey and a lump of sugar, and add some salt and white wine.

Aves o carnes en almendrado
BIRDS OR MEAT IN ALMOND SAUCE
—

Grind together clean roasted almonds, a slice of toasted bread, two hard-cooked egg yolks, parsley, onions, and finely chopped garlic (understand that you should only use two or three cloves at a time).

Parboil the mixture, then add the broth the poultry or meats were cooked in.

Then season it with cloves, cinnamon, and capers, and add wine, vinegar, and a spoonful of sugar.

Let the sauce thicken before placing the cooked poultry or meats in it.

Aves o carnero en estofado
BRAISED BIRDS OR LAMB
—

Stuff the birds or lamb with ham, cloves, pepper, oregano, garlic, halved almonds, and raisins: begin cooking and add more ground spices, salt, lard, water, and good vinegar. Then cover the container with a plate and seal the edges with cornmeal paste.

In another pot, cook seeded tomatoes, frying them later in lard. Put the chicken or lamb in this sauce when they're finished, [then] sprinkle with toasted bread crumbs and a little wine at the end.

∾

Capon al horno
BAKED CAPON
—

For the capon make a paste or stuffing of five eggs, half a pound of sugar, cloves, cinnamon, pepper, saffron, a piece of ground hard biscuit, raisins, and almonds.

Mix well and fry in seasoned lard. Stuff the capons with it. Sew up the opening. Put [them] in a greased pan and place in the oven to bake.

CODORNICES · QUAIL

Codornices a la española
SPANISH-STYLE QUAIL
—

After plucking and gutting the quail, stuff them with the following: chopped cooked mushrooms, green onions, parsley, and thyme. Mix together with a good-sized piece of butter, salt, and the juice of a lemon. Fill them with this stuffing, and cover the stuffing with a crust of bread. After closing the vent, coat them with lard or melted butter, and bread with finely ground crumbs. After this, coat them with beaten eggs, whites and yolks, seasoned well with salt and pepper; coat a second time with a generous helping of bread crumbs, and place them in a baking pan with a little butter or lard to bake in the oven.

You can also roast the quail without breading by coating them well with butter and adding a little water to keep them from burning, basting continuously so they will stay juicy.

᠎∾

Empiñada para pollos ú otras aves
PINEAPPLE SAUCE FOR CHICKENS OR OTHER POULTRY

—

Grind pineapple, tomatoes, toasted garlic, bread toasted in lard, cinnamon, and cloves. Put it all [together] to fry, then add water to make a broth and season [it] with salt.

Put quartered hens or chicken to cook in the pineapple sauce.

ESCABECHE · PICKLED DISHES
Escabeche de gallina
PICKLED HEN

—

Gut and clean the hens, then slice into even pieces. Cook them in a saucepan with water and salt to taste. When done, take out the best pieces and put them in a colander so they can drain well. Dip each piece in beaten egg and fry in very hot lard in a frying pan.

Make a sauce of very finely chopped onion fried by itself in very little lard, and when it starts to brown add a tomato or two, letting it fry before adding a tablespoon of flour. Stir it well, then add hot water, pepper, oregano, and salt. Let the sauce season well before putting the chicken in.

The same sauce can be used for cod cakes.

Advice: with the broth from the hens, make a soup using the pieces that weren't fried.[1]

---

1. While Pinedo called this recipe an *escabeche,* the recipe lacks the normal bay leaf and vinegar ingredients that would characterize it as a pickled dish. This may have been an oversight in her recording of the recipe.—*Translator*

Escabeche
PICKLING SAUCE

—

Make a marinade with wine or vinegar, sprigs of thyme, basil, and marjoram, bay leaves, and other ingredients to remove the bad taste of some meats, or for preserving them, or for fish or other dishes.

FRICASÉ · FRICASSEE

Fricasa de pollos a la española
SPANISH-STYLE CHICKEN FRICASSEE

—

After gutting and cleaning the chickens, cut in pieces not too small, then fry them in fresh lard and salt. At the same time that you fry the chickens, fry two chopped onions, two shallots, finely chopped garlic cloves, and a cup of sliced mushrooms.

When done, add a half cup of olives, some chopped parsley, half a dozen stuffed olives, and some oil. Mix well, add a cup of tomato juice, ground toasted bread crumbs, thyme or oregano, salt, and pepper.

Stir the mixture carefully so it doesn't stick to the pan.

Moisten the stew with boiling water and cover the pan, cooking the fricassee over a moderate fire until ready. Thicken the sauce by pouring egg yolks mixed with milk on top.

GALLINAS · STEWING HENS

Gallinas rellenas
STUFFED STEWING HENS

—

For each hen, take a pound of sugar made into clear syrup. Add to this four ground biscuits, cinnamon, saffron, pine nuts, toasted almonds in pieces, eight beaten eggs, four ounces of grated aged cheese, and a little white wine. Mix it all together and put on the fire until the eggs are cooked.

Parboil the hens with wine and salt, then fill them with this stuffing. Put in the roaster, grease with butter, and let brown in the oven.

GUAJOLOTES · TURKEYS

Guajolote en clamole castellano
TURKEY IN CASTILIAN SAUCE

—

Toast pine nuts, hazelnuts, walnuts, and some avocado leaves. Heat deveined ancho chile until it is highly toasted. Grind it all with a little toasted biscuit and fry in lard. Then add the broth the turkey was cooked in.

Let the broth simmer until the flavors blend and it thickens, and add the salt at the very end so the *mole* does not separate.

Guajolote asado y relleno
ROAST AND STUFFED TURKEY

—

Clean the turkey and stuff it. It can be stuffed with a *picadillo* of all kinds of meats mixed with sausages or, if you like, roast chestnuts.

88

Guajolote en mole gallego
TURKEY IN GALICIAN SAUCE

———

Fry deveined ancho chile and grind with some toasted almonds, toasted sesame seed, and walnuts if you like, all three things in equal quantities.

Fry it all in lard, adding some boiling water and a small lump of sugar. Put in the raw turkey pieces, and let cook until the sauce thickens. When the flavors in the *mole* have blended, add the salt so it doesn't separate.

Mole de guajolote o pavo
MEXICAN TURKEY SAUCE

———

Toast two pounds of almonds, and grind them when hot and dry. Next take a little coriander seed and toast with an equal part of anise; add a little pepper, some cloves and cinnamon, a piece of well-toasted corn tortilla, and a head of roasted garlic. Grind all of these together after the almonds.

Next take a half pound of dried chiles browned in lard, and grind with the almonds and spices. Now fry some fresh tomatoes until they come apart in the pan. Then put in some hot water and add the turkey with some pork. Cook it over a gentle fire, add a little sugar, but do not cover the pot. Salt is added just before serving.

Serve in a plate, garnished with a little toasted sesame seed.

ᦇ

Palomas guisadas
STEWED DOVES

—

After gutting the doves, fry in olive oil with a sprig of chervil, two dozen French boiling onions, a whole head of garlic, a cup of mushrooms, salt, pepper, toasted bread, and enough water to cook them.

∾

Pasteles calientes de pollos por la señorita Angelina
MISS ANGELINA'S HOT CHICKEN PIES

—

Make a very rich puff pastry. Stretch it with a rolling pin in an even layer, cut with a mold in pieces about one and a half inches [large] in half-moon shapes and in circles, and put in the oven to bake.

Next, make a fricassee for pie. After cleaning the chickens, slice them and fry in very hot lard with onion, finely chopped peeled and seeded tomatoes, and two tablespoons of flour. Stir and turn the chickens carefully so as not to mash them, adding a good handful of chopped parsley and boiling water.

Cook the fricassee over a low flame, without letting it become too soupy. Then put it in the pie and decorate [it] with the baked pastry circles just before carrying it to the table.

Pastel de codornices
QUAIL PIE
—

Clean and stuff the quail. Line a dish with a nice rich pie pastry. In the bottom put some slices of salt pork, some cooked eggs, some butter, and pepper. Then dust the quail, sprinkling with chopped parsley and lemon juice and small pieces of butter coated with toasted flour, and moisten with sherry. Put everything in the dish and add a cup of broth.

Cover the quail with another sheet of pastry, and spread the pastry with syrup before putting in the oven.

Pasteles de pollos y pichones
CHICKEN AND SQUAB PIE
—

Make a mince of veal, bacon, and ham. Fry the picadillo in hot lard with three or four medium onions, plenty of mushrooms cut in large strips, two apples, artichoke bottoms, four tomatoes, oregano, pepper, and salt, and let it all cook together until the flavors develop.

Separately cook the chickens and squabs a little, the chicken chopped in small pieces but the squab cut only in half.

Cover a pie pan with a layer of pastry, put in a layer of the picadillo, then the pieces of meat, and cover with more picadillo. Another way to make this is to put another layer of pastry on top to cover everything, and put the pie in the oven.

PICADILLO · MINCE

Picadillo de ave
MINCED FOWL

—

Chop the remnants of the bird. Place in a casserole with a good piece of butter with a spoonful of flour dissolved in cream. Add salt, pepper, grated nutmeg, and raw egg yolks to the picadillo. Butter a serving dish, put in the picadillo, and put it on the stove.

PICHONES · SQUAB

Pichones con puntas de espárragos
SQUAB WITH ASPARAGUS TIPS

—

Cut the squab in four pieces and fry them in lard with salt. When they are half browned, add a chopped onion and garlic, and then continue to fry, adding two tablespoons of flour.

Turn and stir the squab well, adding boiling water and a tablespoon of vinegar. Sprinkle with salt and pepper, and then add cooked asparagus tips.

POLLOS · CHICKEN

Pollos gachupínes
GACHUPÍN CHICKEN

—

Fry some garlic until golden. Take out the garlic, and put in the un-cooked chicken cut into frying pieces.

Chop plenty of onions and put [them] in the pan with olives, pars-ley, a little water, a slice of bread fried in olive oil, oregano, and pepper.

Chop raw ham and add to the broth, and let it cook over a slow fire.[2]

Pollos rellenos de mole
CHICKEN STUFFED WITH *MOLE* SAUCE

—

Grind deveined pasilla and ancho chiles with cloves, pepper, and roasted tomatoes. Fry these in lard.

Roast pork loins. Cut into small pieces and then add them to the *mole* with some toasted and ground sesame seed, seasoning with salt.

Stuff the raw chickens or hens with this *picadillo* and roast them. When you serve, coat them with butter and serve on lettuce hearts.

Pollos guisados
STEWED CHICKEN

—

Fry two chickens and two squabs. When they are half done, add two gar-lic cloves, sliced onion, tomatoes, olive, mushrooms, raisins, chopped parsley, [and] flour or toasted bread, adding boiling water with oregano, then leave it to simmer over a very low fire.

2. *Gachupín* is an offensive adjective describing a Spanish-born individual living in Mexico.—*Translator*

Pollos enchilados rellenos
CHILIED STUFFED CHICKEN

———

Chop a piece of pork loin as if making a *longaniza* sausage, and mix it with a little deveined and toasted ancho chile with some spices and vinegar. Put in some chopped ham, some *chorizo*, and almonds. Mix it together to stuff the chickens.

Put them in a baking pan greased with butter or lard.

Pollos en pebre gachupín
CHICKEN IN *GACHUPÍN* SAUCE

———

Fry onions, parsley, garlic [with] a cup of oil and another of vinegar. Put in the chicken pieces, some hot peppers, ground spices, [and] salt.

Put on the fire until it becomes tender and the flavors develop.

∾

Zorzales guisados
STEWED THRUSHES

———

Put a casserole on the fire with fresh butter. Fry the thrushes or birds like them along with some truffles, salt, and pepper.

When the birds are browned, add well-washed chopped intestines, a bay leaf, garlic, chopped parsley, and a tablespoon of flour. Let this fry for a while, moistening the stew with two glasses of champagne or white wine. Then cover the casserole well so the steam doesn't escape.

When you serve the stew, add a few drops of lemon.

CARNE

MEAT

ALBÓNDIGAS · MEATBALLS

Albóndigas a la española
SPANISH-STYLE MEATBALLS

—

Chop equal parts of raw veal and chicken breasts; when well chopped, add bread crumbs moistened with broth and egg yolks and whites, onion, parsley, tarragon, pepper, salt, and a piece of butter the size of an egg. Mix everything together with your hands, and form the meatballs, putting them in a boiling broth.

Albóndigas a la alemana
GERMAN-STYLE MEATBALLS

—

Chop veal or pork until it's reduced to a paste. Also chop a small piece of lard, with onion, parsley, nutmeg, pepper, paprika, salt, thyme, two handfuls of bread crumbs, and a tablespoon of savory dry flour.

Mix everything with your hands, and make larger than usual meatballs, and put them in boiling water.

Add parsley and finely chopped green onion to the broth.

Albóndigas a la italiana
ITALIAN-STYLE MEATBALLS
—

Chop some pork leg meat well, add garlic, a little clove, parsley, mint, pepper, raw eggs, cheese, sliced bread, some well-ground bread crumbs. Put in a broth seasoned with saffron, clove, and salt.

The sauce is made with garlic cloves fried in lard, onion, and tomatoes: when these are fried, add the broth, and while this is boiling, make the meatballs and add them to the broth, and cook over a gentle fire, and then add the saffron and the pepper.

Albóndigas de cataluña
CATALAN MEATBALLS
—

Chop some pork, add some chopped ham, parsley, mint, cilantro, garlic, chopped onions, eggs, grated and soaked bread, clove, pepper, saffron, and vinegar, and, if you like, add some cumin.

Next make the sauce as you've been told, and thicken it with egg and bread as usual.[1]

1. While Pinedo says to make the sauce "as you've been told," her preceding recipes do not include a standard sauce instruction, nor does her salsa section contain a recipe specifically for either Catalan dishes or meatballs. This may indicate that the recipe was transcribed from an oral instruction, or lifted from another printed source.—*Translator*

Albóndigas españolas a la alemana
SPANISH MEATBALLS IN THE GERMAN STYLE

—

Take a quarter loaf of milk bread, and moisten it with water or milk.

Put a tablespoon of dry flour, two eggs (yolks and whites), and the moistened bread, well wrung by your hands, in a soup bowl. Add parsley, finely chopped thyme, pepper, nutmeg, and salt.

Beat this mixture with a spoon: if the batter is too thick, it can be thinned with a tablespoon of fat from the broth. Bring the broth to a boil just before serving, and then drop the batter into the broth with a coffee spoon. After simmering, the meatballs will rise to the surface, and will be ready to serve.

The Germans call these sponge meatballs.

ASADOS · ROASTS

Asado de buey
ROAST BEEF

—

Take a piece of meat and sprinkle both sides with salt and pepper. Put it in a flat baking dish in a very hot oven, taking care to keep the oven at the same temperature while roasting; otherwise the roast will become tough and dry.

When the roast starts to brown, add boiling water.

During the second half of the roasting time, it is important to baste frequently. When done, mix the meat juices with the basting liquid.

Asado de buey a la mexicana en asador
MEXICAN-STYLE GRILLED BEEF

Grilled meat is the most flavorful, and this is the most primitive style in which to prepare it.

Take large slices of the meat, fold them, and thread on a four-sided iron rod with a point on the end. Put it over some coals and watch it continuously, turning the meats so they stay moist yet get well browned.

Asado de carnero
ROAST LAMB

The leg of lamb is the best part. Lard with pieces of bacon and garlic cloves sliced in fine strips.

Dampen the leg with water, and rub all sides with salt, pepper, and flour.

Put it into a blazing fire, keeping the fire lively from the beginning.

When the roast starts to color, give it a turn as needed; add boiling water to baste it with a spoon as needed. Then moderate the fire and let it roast slowly.

Asado de pecho de ternero
ROAST VEAL BREAST

Cut the breast into a square shape, then lift up the part over the ribs, cut lengthwise to split it open, stuff it, and sew it up.

Then put it in a casserole with one or two cups of broth or water, adding onion, parsley, pepper, and salt, then let it simmer until done.

When done, take it out and put in a roasting pan; put it in the oven to finish.

Asado de lechón
ROAST SUCKLING PIG [1]

—

Prepare a young pig and stuff it. As soon as the pig begins to cook, rub it with olive oil to give it a pretty golden color.

Asado de lechón
ROAST SUCKLING PIG [2]

—

Scald and carefully clean the meat. Let it rest in water with vinegar and salt for eight hours, then suspend it in the air to drain. After stuffing, cover the pig with slices of bacon or rub it well with salt and flour and grease well with butter. When it begins to take on color, add some water with which you can baste the pig.

A roast suckling pig cooks for four hours.

ᏋᏋ

Barbacoa (carne asada en hoyo o cabeza tatenada)
BARBECUE (MEAT ROASTED IN A PIT, OR BARBECUED HEAD)

—

Cut the head off close to the nape of the neck and pierce the skin all over, larding it with whole dry chiles, garlic cloves, pieces of onion, and fat pork or ham marinated for twelve hours in chile, garlic, vinegar, salt, ginger, [and] all types of spices, adding lime slices. Also, season the tongue with as much oregano as you can.

Once the head you want to barbecue is prepared, get the pit ready. It should be at least three feet deep, burning well with a lively fire and even-sized stones on the bottom. When you see that the stones and the pit are red hot, take out the rest of the wood and remove half the stones. Wrap the head in a bag, put it in the hole, place the hot stones on the top and sides, and cover it all with a layer of mint. On top of this put a layer of matting or a sack, and then ashes, and cover with dirt. The barbecue stays in the pit all night, and when everything is ready for lunch, take out the roast head, which is delicious, and serve with appropriate sauces.

∾

Buey (costillas) a la moda
BEEF RIBS À LA MODE
—

Prepare the ribs, and lard with strips of ham seasoned with garlic, clove, cinnamon, ginger, salt, and pepper. Line the bottom of a casserole with slices of ham and beef, put four parsnips on top, five large roasted onions stuck with three cloves, two bay leaves, a little thyme, and a bunch of parsley.

Tie the ribs with a string, and put in the prepared casserole. Cover with ham and vegetable garnishes. Put in a few spoonfuls of broth and bring to a boil. Then slowly cook it over a low fire for three hours or less, until the meat is tender.

When done, pass some of the broth through a sieve, remove the fat, and make a reduction to coat the ribs.

CARNE SECA · DRIED BEEF

Carne seca a la española
SPANISH-STYLE DRIED BEEF
—

Rinse the dried meat in fresh water and put in a roasting pan to roast in the oven. When done, let it cool before pounding it. Thoroughly pound [it], then shred it with your hands and fry in four ounces of lard with two tablespoons of flour and garlic, and a good red-chile sauce with a little oregano.

Stew until well seasoned before serving. Keep in mind that it is very important for it to be very moist.

Carne de vaca en lonja (beefsteak) asada a la parilla
GRILLED BEEFSTEAK

———

Take a good slice from the short loin and pound it on both sides, then season with salt and pepper.

Put it over some good coals and grill it with care, turning as needed so it cooks on both sides.

When done, place on the serving dish and sprinkle with chopped parsley. Cover and put in the oven a few minutes to be sure it is hot when served.

Carne de vaca en lonja (beefsteak) (en la sartén)
PAN-FRIED BEEFSTEAK

———

Take a good thick piece of the short loin or other desired cut. Pound on both sides and season with salt and pepper. Grease the frying pan with fresh butter, then put the meat in the pan. Put it over a high flame for a few minutes, turning it several times, then put the frying pan in the corner of the stove where it will cook slowly. Serve it in a dish lined with strips of thinly sliced lemon and triangles of toasted bread, and sprinkle with finely chopped parsley.

Carne seca de ternera en tasajos
DRIED VEAL STRIPS

—

Remove the bones and cut large strips with a knife. Salt [it], put in some lemon slices, and let sit for several hours.

Hang it on a cord in the sun, and when dry keep it for use when you wish.

Carne asada en la olla de los misioneros
MISSIONARY-STYLE POT ROAST

—

Take a good piece of well-marbled meat and lard it with small pieces of fat and garlic.

Grease the bottom of the pot with lard and put in the meat.

Cover the pot with an iron lid and put some hot coals on top.

When the meat is half done, add a sauce of toasted chile and oregano, turn the meat in the sauce, then cover again with the same lid. A small amount of sauce can be made with the pan juices.

Carne estofada a la española
SPANISH-STYLE BRAISED MEAT

—

Cut the meat in chunks of three or four inches, wash [them], and put in the pot without lard, with two chopped garlic cloves and salt to taste. Cover the marmite and cook on a good fire. When the meat is half done, add two tomatoes, two or three seeded chiles, and two onions, cut into quarters when the onion is half done. Add one or two tablespoons of flour and some hot water, then stir it together and cover.

Keep the marmite tightly covered while the stew is cooking so the steam doesn't escape.

Carnes asadas recalentadas
WARMED-UP ROAST MEATS

All roast meat should be reheated without boiling, otherwise it becomes very tough.

Cold roast beef cut into slices can be heated in tomato sauce or in hot sauce. After heating the sauce, put in the meat.

∾

Patitas de cerdo en adobo
MARINATED PIGS' FEET

Cook the feet and remove the large bones. Roll them in flour, dip them in beaten egg, fry them, and then put them in a broth.

Finely grind some deveined and well-washed ancho chiles, a head of garlic, and a little cumin. Fry it all with a little of the broth the feet were cooked in, mixing it with some water. Season with salt [and] pepper, and sprinkle with oregano.

Put the feet in this broth until the flavors meld.

CHORIZO · SAUSAGE

Chorizo a la mexicana
MEXICAN-STYLE SAUSAGE

Finely mince some pork. If the meat is lean, supplement it with fat chopped as finely as possible. The day before making the *chorizos*, thoroughly wash a good quantity of red pasilla chiles in cold water, and let them soak. The following day empty the chiles into a sieve and drain them of all the water.

Grind the chiles in the *metate* and soak them with vinegar. As you grind the chiles, also grind in some peeled garlic cloves.

When the sauce is ready, flavor it with salt and oregano, pour into the meat and fat, and mix well with several turns.

When the sausage meat is prepared, fill the casing, which already has been bleached for this purpose. Tie both ends of each *chorizo* with string, making them the size that you wish. Then hang them on a string so they can air-dry in a cool place.

Chorizos fritos
FRIED SAUSAGES
—

Fry small *chorizos* in lard, and when they are done and partly browned, serve them with croutons of bread fried in the same lard.

To improve the flavor of the *chorizos,* some cooks add a few drops of good vinegar and a little bit of salt.

Longanizas are served over grated potatoes.

CLAMOLE · STEW

Clamole castellano
CASTILIAN STEW
—

Cook a hen and a clean pork loin [with] *longaniza, chorizo,* and *butifarra* sausages [see Ingredients and Procedures section—*Translator*].

Clamole de palacio
PALACE STEW
—

Devein and toast three pounds of pasilla chiles; mix with a half pound of cocoa and another half pound of almonds, both well toasted, and a half ounce of cinnamon.

Grind the chile with roasted, peeled tomatoes, then add the cocoa, cinnamon, and almonds. Fry it all in lard, then dissolve with boiling water.

Add to the meat and sausages. Season with some sugar. Add salt after it has boiled so it will not be too thick.

In some lard, separately brown deveined pasilla chiles, a little sesame, peeled almonds, and cleaned peanuts.

Fry these last ingredients until they've absorbed all the fat, then add the ground chile and, when fried, add the chicken and pieces of pork loin, with broth, and season with salt.

COCHINILLOS · SUCKLING PIG

Cochinillo en adobo
MARINATED SUCKLING PIG
—

Make a marinade with toasted and seeded ancho chiles, cumin, and oregano; if you like, you can add some bread crumbs soaked in vinegar and water, so that after the meat cooks it will thicken the broth.

Put in the whole suckling pig, or cut into large pieces. Marinate for seven, eight, or twenty-four hours, according to size. This way you can serve it right after stewing, but it is most savory when the fire has reduced almost all or most of the broth.

COSTILLAS · RIBS AND CHOPS

Costillas de carnero asadas y panadas
BREADED AND ROASTED LAMB CHOPS

———

Dip the chops in oil or melted lard, then beat some egg yolks with parsley and finely chopped shallots, and season with salt and pepper.

Cover the chops with the beaten eggs, and crumble on top as many hand-ground bread crumbs as each can absorb, then wrap each chop in larded paper, put in a roasting pan in the oven, and let roast on a low fire for an hour.

Costillas de puerco fresco con setas
FRESH PORK CHOPS WITH MUSHROOMS

———

Prepare the chops as though they were to be roasted on the grill; but these are fried in pork fat without salt or olive oil. Fry them in a skillet, turning them several times and seasoning both sides with salt and pepper.

Remove them from the skillet when they are golden brown. Then put some sliced mushrooms in the drippings that are left, with onions, parsley, finely chopped basil, a cup of white wine, and a half cup of hot water.

Put the chops in the same dish and cover with the sauce.

∾

Enrollado
BEEF ROLL

———

Cut and chop beef mixed with pork and spice with vinegar, chile, oregano, pepper, and salt.

Put the mince on a pounded slice of beef or a clean piece of pork rind, roll it up and tie with a strong cord, and put it to cook.

ESTOFADOS · BRAISES

Estofado a la española
SPANISH-STYLE BRAISE

———

Gut and clean the hens, then cut them in small pieces: arrange them in a casserole with a layer of hen pieces and a layer of finely chopped onion, one or two cloves of garlic cut into very fine strips, salt, pepper, seeded and peeled tomatoes, and raisins.

Sprinkle each layer with sugar, and when you've put in all the layers, add a cup of claret.

Cover the casserole very well so the steam will not escape when it simmers.

Let the braise cook at a very low flame for three or four hours.

Estofado a la española por Carmencita
CARMEN'S SPANISH-STYLE BRAISE

———

After cleaning the hens, cut into small pieces.

Arrange in a pot a layer of hen, covering with another layer of chopped onion, some raisins, salt, pepper, sugar, peeled and seeded tomatoes, strained tomatoes if you have them, [and] very little garlic.

Sprinkle the layer with a good vinegar, but not too much.

Arrange another layer of hen; cover it in the same way until the pot is full, adding half a cup of water to moisten the birds.

Cover the pot well and let simmer over a low flame for two or three hours.

Advice: this stew can also be made with lamb ribs.

༄

Lengua enchilada
TONGUE IN CHILE SAUCE

—

Wash the tongue, then cook it in some lightly salted water so that it doesn't come out bland. Peel it and slice it.

Next put the tongue in a thick red-chile sauce, adding some sliced onions, olives, oregano, salt, olive oil, and vinegar.

You can thicken the sauce with clean, toasted, ground walnuts or syrup, if you wish. Serve it cold.

LIEBRE · HARE

Liebre civet a la francesa
FRENCH-STYLE JUGGED HARE

—

Cut the hare or rabbit in pieces, [and] put it in a casserole with butter, a handful of herbs, ham, the liver, artichoke bottoms, and mushrooms. Put it all on the fire.

Add a little flour dissolved in broth, salt, pepper, and a glass of white wine or champagne.

When everything is cooked, just before serving, put a garnish on top made with the rabbit liver that was cooked in the same broth.

Liebre enchilada
RABBIT IN CHILE SAUCE

—

Cut the rabbit in small pieces. Fry in very hot fresh lard with small pieces of pork fat.

Fry over a quick fire, and when it begins to brown, add some chopped onion, garlic, and salt.

Let it cook, then add tomatoes, olives, chopped mushrooms, one or two spoonfuls of flour, and powdered oregano. Cover it with a chile sauce, leaving the casserole covered, and cook it over a moderate flame.

∾

Manchamanteles
STEW THAT STAINS THE TABLECLOTH

—

Take some ripe tomatoes and remove the seeds. Grind them with soaked toasted dry chiles, cinnamon, and pepper. After they are ground, fry in lard, mix with warm water, and add chickens or pork, cooked sausages, olives, vinegar, salt, a lump of sugar, yams, or peanuts.

∾

Manitas de ternera
CALVES' FEET

—

Cook the feet for three hours, and when perfectly done, drain and cool them.

Dress them with oil, vinegar, pepper, mustard, shallots, parsley, and basil, all very finely minced.

MANTECA · LARD

In the best kitchens, they use back fat for pastry for pies, empanadas, and stews.

A mixture of pork and beef lard is very good, much better if you mix it with back fat.

You must always employ fresh lard of a good quality for cooking.

Manteca frita en baño de María
LARD RENDERED IN A *BAIN-MARIE*[2]

———

Pork lard should be rendered at a moderate flame. Let it cool after it turns a pretty golden color, strain it, and keep [it] in a clay jar. Warm it a little if you can add some good back fat that has been rendered separately. This mixture makes good stews and pastry.

Manteca frita
RENDERED LARD

———

When you want good white lard, cut it in pieces or cubes that are very small. Put it in a pan over boiling water in a marmite. In this way, melt the lard, strain it, and keep it. In the same way, you [can] prepare fat from geese, ducks, or hens. These you use to prepare different sauces, condiments, and stuffings.

———

2. The *bain-marie* is a French technique used to cook delicate dishes by placing the cooking container in a water bath. That she has chosen a Continental technique to render lard speaks strongly about her sophisticated style of cooking.—*Translator*

MOLE

Mole de carnero
LAMB *MOLE*

—

Toast, devein, and fry equal quantities of ancho and pasilla chiles; then toast the seeds of the same chiles and grind them with peanuts, clove, and cinnamon. Put this on to fry, and break up the chiles in it. Then when it all comes together, add hot water and salt. Take great care that it does not get watery, and then add the cooked meat and let it simmer.

MORCILLA · BLOOD SAUSAGE

Morcilla negra a la española
SPANISH-STYLE BLACK BLOOD SAUSAGE

—

Black blood sausage is made with pig's blood.

Take the blood from the pig and put it into a pot. Put in a spoonful of salt. This will set the blood even if it is hot. The blood needs to be beaten and then passed through a sieve before it coagulates.

Peel an onion and cut in small cubes. Get the best lard from the inside of the pig and chop it in very small squares with two ground garlic cloves, finely minced mint, two teaspoons of red-chile seeds, and pepper.

Mix all of this with the blood, and add very fresh, rich milk. For two half liters of blood, add two small cups of milk.

Stir, and when it reaches a good consistency, fill casings that have been properly cleaned and prepared.

Tie both ends of each sausage with a string, making each the size you wish.

Place inside a casserole a few at a time, in very hot water, but not hot enough for them to boil. Carefully turn them from time to time, and add cold water to the casserole so they do not burst. Let them cook until the blood coagulates firmly, which you can tell if no blood drops come out when you prick them.

Remove from the water and hang them to air-dry.

Olla bueno
GOOD STEW

Wash the meat and put it in the pot with boiling water and salt. Remove the scum and add garbanzos, one or two whole heads of garlic, cloves, ham, pigs' feet, a piece of jowl, some sausages, poultry, a cabbage, a squash, peas, and onions. Season with a little saffron.

Olla podrida a la española
SPANISH STEW

Put some water in a pot for the stew, and add a piece of lamb or veal, a slice of raw ham, and some bird or game giblets. Put it on the fire, skim any scum, [and] add a piece of salt pork, garbanzos, and salt to taste if needed.

Add to the pot any vegetables you wish—young squash, green beans, corn on the cob, pears, half a cabbage, potatoes, leeks, onions, two heads of garlic, tomatoes, and parsley.

When serving, place the meats and vegetables on one large platter.

Pastel de carne seca
DRIED BEEF CASSEROLE

After roasting the dried meat in the Spanish style, shred it and mash it well.

Make a sauce with four sliced medium onions, four large tomatoes, olives, raisins, powdered oregano, and cumin. When the sauce is half fried, add a tablespoon of flour, and let it fry a few minutes, stirring the sauce carefully so you don't crush the onion. Then pour in a cup of thick red-chile sauce and the meat. Let the sauce cook until well seasoned before baking the pie.

Line a pie pan with a corn dough and fill with the stew, covering it in sequence with a sheet of pastry dough, brushed with syrup.

These pies should be left in the oven only long enough to give the pastry a beautiful golden color.

RIÑONES · KIDNEYS

Riñones de carnero con vino blanco
LAMB KIDNEYS WITH WHITE WINE

Divide the kidneys in two pieces along their length. Cut them in thin slices and fry in fresh hot lard with plenty of sliced mushrooms and garlic.

Flavor with salt, pepper, and grated nutmeg.

When the kidneys are well browned, add a handful of parsley and a spoonful of flour. Stir them vigorously while pouring on boiling water and a cup of wine.

SANDWICHES

Sandwiches de pâte de fois gras
LIVER-PASTE SANDWICHES

––

Cut slices of bread very thin and in a semicircular shape. Spread the slices with butter and a little French mustard, and then the pâté de foie gras.

Cover this with another slice of bread spread the same way.

Arrange the sandwiches on the serving dish and cover with a napkin so they don't dry out.

If you serve mustard with the sandwiches, you don't need to put it on the bread.

Otro sandwich
ANOTHER SANDWICH

––

Chop a cooked beef tongue, season with salt and white pepper, some spoonfuls of hot sauce, two tablespoons of oil, finely chopped chervil or other herbs, and mix together with a half teaspoon of French mustard.

SESOS · BRAINS

Sesos de ternera
VEAL BRAINS

—

Drain the blood from the brains in hot water and remove the membranes that cover them, then cook them in water with vinegar, salt, and pepper.

Put a pot on the fire with lard, and when it is hot, add four tablespoons of flour, let it brown well, then add a spoonful of broth and another of wine, salt, pepper, green onion, and chopped parsley.

Simmer and reduce the sauce, then pour it over the brains on a serving platter.

Sesos en salsa
BRAINS IN SAUCE

—

Put them in hot water to clean out the blood, and when clean, put in cool water, then in boiling water with lemon juice.

Make a good sauce using a good olive oil with tomato, poached artichoke bottoms, green onion, chopped parsley, salt, pepper, and marjoram.

Put the brains in, cut in pieces, and flavor with wine or a few drops of vinegar.

Sesos de ternera en salsa
VEAL BRAINS IN SAUCE

—

After deblooding and cleaning the brains, braise in simmering water with lemon juice.

Make a sauce in butter with sliced onions, cooked and sliced artichoke bottoms, cooked lobster, chopped parsley, squares of toasted bread, a bay leaf, pepper, salt, lemon juice, and the brains cut in pieces.

VERDURAS Y MAÍZ

VEGETABLE AND CORN DISHES

Alcachofas
ARTICHOKES

Remove the leaves from around the artichokes, then soak them.

Simmer the artichokes with the heads down, about one-third covered in the water. Hermetically seal the casserole with a piece of linen and put the cover on this. Put it on the fire, which should be fairly hot. The steam will penetrate the artichokes and preserve their natural flavor.

You can use one-half water and one-half olive oil [for cooking the artichokes]. If you like them cold, serve with oil, vinegar, salt, and pepper.

Alcachofas en vinagre
ARTICHOKES IN VINEGAR

Cut the tips from the artichokes and cook them with plenty of chopped garlic and salt. After removing the choke, put a pot on the fire in which you've put a quart of oil for each dozen artichokes, first frying tomatoes in the oil.

When the tomatoes are done, put in the artichokes; add a little vinegar, grated bread, and salt. Cook over a good fire, covering the pot well. Let it simmer until the broth is nearly gone.

Serve these hot.

Arroz guisado a la española
STEWED SPANISH RICE

—

Melt two ounces of fresh butter in a casserole. Add two or three chopped cloves of garlic. Remove them as soon as they take on color, and when the fat is quite hot, add a cup of well-washed rice and salt.

Stir the rice continuously while it is on the fire, and when it begins to turn golden, add half a chopped onion and, a few moments later, a chopped tomato. Stir it all constantly, until the tomato starts to dry, then add two ladles of broth or boiling water.

Cover the casserole well and place it on one side of the stove. Let it cook slowly for three-quarters of an hour. If the rice becomes too dry, add a little hot water, stirring the spoon carefully on the bottom of the casserole so as not to crush the rice.

Serve on a dish, and cover the rice with fried eggs on the serving platter.

∿

Berengenas a la tortera
BAKED EGGPLANT

—

Cut the eggplants in half and remove the pulp. Cut them up finely with a little chopped garlic.

Put everything in a pot with butter and let it stew.

Put the eggplant shells in a baking dish, fill with the mince, and bake in the oven. Dress them and serve hot.

CALABAZAS · SQUASH

Calabacitas rellenas
STUFFED SQUASH

———

Hollow out both ends with the end of a scoop or a cooking spoon, stuff them with a *picadillo* or with cheese, cover the opening with pieces of turnip cut in the shape of a cork, place in a pot lined with slices of ham, cover with some broth, and cook over a low fire.

Serve with tomato sauce.

Calabacitas en mantequilla
SQUASH IN BUTTER

———

Cut the squash in quarters, and cook in water.

When done, take them out of the water, leaving just a little.

Serve them with butter, grated cheese, salt, and pepper.

Calabacitas a la mexicana
MEXICAN-STYLE SQUASH

———

Slice the squash and simmer in lightly salted water. Put them in a napkin to drain all the water they contain. Then dip in beaten egg and fry in very hot lard. When done, elegantly make a layer of squash, cover with plenty of grated cheese and butter, and continue to layer, finishing with a layer of cheese.

Make these layers on a platter, which is put in the oven so they can be served very hot.

CEBOLLAS · ONIONS

Cebollas en la cazuela
ONIONS IN A CASSEROLE

———

Choose some medium-sized onions and peel them, putting them in the bottom of a casserole with a little butter. Then add a glass of water, salt, pepper, and a little sugar. Cook on a high fire until the sauce has almost disappeared. Then put them in a serving dish; splash with a few drops of vinegar, a little chopped parsley, and the water from the casserole. Let the sauce simmer, and pour it over the onions, which should be served hot.

∾

Chicharos verdes a la española
SPANISH-STYLE GREEN PEAS

———

Put a good piece of lard in a casserole and, when good and hot, add a finely chopped green onion, one or two tablespoons of tomato, salt, pepper, and a tablespoon of sugar.

Let the tomato simmer for a few minutes, then add the freshly shelled peas.

Sauté over a low fire, stirring so they do not stick to the bottom of the pan. Add a little water, cover the pot, and let it cook for a while on low heat.

∾

Chilaquiles tapatios a la mexicana
GUADALAJARA-STYLE TORTILLA CASSEROLE

Fry pork and sausage with red pasilla chiles, and tomatoes if you like.

Make a layer of meat and another of corn tortillas. Cover with chile that contains some fat, and make layers until the dish is full.

Put grated cheese and olives on top.

Chilaquiles a la mexicana
MEXICAN-STYLE TORTILLA CASSEROLE

Fry ground chile, and when it is almost ready, add the amount of water that seems right.

Boil until it reduces to a sauce, add some shredded day-old tortillas, bring it to a boil for a second time, and when it is almost dry, beat some eggs into the casserole and add grated cheese and olives.

If you wish, serve with fried sausage or macaroni.

Chilaquiles con camarones secos
TORTILLA CASSEROLE WITH DRIED SHRIMP

Fry the chile sauce in lard and add boiling water.

When it has reduced to a sauce, add cleaned shrimp, fried potatoes cut in cubes, olives, oregano, and salt.

Simmer until nearly dry, beat in some eggs, and add grated cheese.

CHILES

Chiles rellenos
STUFFED CHILES [1]

———

Prepare the egg for the chiles: separate the whites from the yolks. Beat the whites with a fork or a wicker spoon, but by no means with a beater.

When the whites are beaten to snowy peaks, add three tablespoons of flour and fold in the eggs to incorporate the flour. The yolks are not added to the whites until the moment the chiles are fried. Take this precaution. The other way makes the batter very thin, and the chiles don't fry well, because they have to be coated well with the egg to come out right.

For fifteen chiles you should use ten eggs. Don't beat the yolks until they are ready to be added to the whites at the moment you fry the chiles. When the yolks are added to the whites, give them half a turn, pouring them on the chiles, turning them in the batter, then putting them in the already hot lard.

Chiles rellenos
STUFFED CHILES [2]

———

With scrambled eggs and cooked artichoke bottoms.

Chiles verdes rellenos
STUFFED GREEN CHILES

—

Choose chiles that are very fresh, wide, and smooth. Roast them over the stove or over good hot coals, watching carefully that they do not burn too much, turning them over on all sides so that they roast evenly.

As soon as they are done, wrap them in a damp napkin and leave them wrapped for six to eight minutes.

After they have set, skin them carefully, being careful not to tear them.

Remove the crown and seed carefully.

Now stuff the chiles with *picadillo*, using a teaspoon.

After the chiles are stuffed with *picadillo*, coat them one at a time in beaten egg, and fry them in enough very hot lard so the chiles float in it.

Note: When roasting chiles over the coals, one must be very careful not to burn them, turning them over with a kitchen fork. Once roasted, they can also be put in a tray of cold water. After peeling them, remove the core and seeds, and drain them for filling, or any other use you wish to make of them.

Chiles rellenos (picadillo)
CHILES STUFFED WITH MINCE

—

Chop or grind in a mortar a good piece of sirloin from which you have carefully removed the nerves.

Next, chop two onions, a cup of mushrooms, two peeled and cored apples, olives chopped or whole: chop everything separately.

Place a frying pan on the fire with a scant tablespoon of lard. Fry four chopped garlic cloves in it. Remove them from the lard as soon as they take on color, and put in the meat and let [it] fry a few minutes before adding the onion, the mushrooms, the apples, a cup of tomato juice, a half cup of well-washed raisins, six unstuffed olives, chopped parsley, oregano, pepper, salt, and a teaspoon of fresh butter.

Let the *picadillo* cook over a low flame for a quarter hour without stirring so the flavors develop well.

Chiles rellenos de camarones
CHILES STUFFED WITH SHRIMP

Fry chopped onion, tomato, garlic, and parsley in lard. Add olive oil, vinegar, pepper, and salt, if necessary, because it should be highly seasoned.

Add the shrimp, then hot water with saffron, cilantro, and fried toast.

Bring it all to a simmer, then stuff the chiles, dip them [in] a batter of eggs, and fry them in lard.

Chiles rellenos de bacalao
CHILES STUFFED WITH SALT COD

You make them the same way you were told to make those with shrimp or crab.

Chiles verdes rellenos con queso
GREEN CHILES STUFFED WITH CHEESE

Slice the cheese not too thin and stuff the chiles; roll them in egg and fry them.

Chiles rellenos con sardina francesa en cajas
CHILES STUFFED WITH CANNED FRENCH SARDINES

—

Prepare the green chiles, then stuff them with whole sardines. Place the chiles decoratively on a large serving dish, then cover them with onions that have been soaked in fresh water and lemon juice; sprinkle them with grated cheese, olives, and some drops of lemon juice and the oil from the sardines.

Chiles rellenos y avinagrados
STUFFED AND VINEGARED CHILES [1]

—

Remove the tops from green chiles as well as the seeds and the veins, being careful not to break them open. Soak them, and leave them to drain.

Next make a mince with a very tender white cabbage, a stalk of very yellow and fresh celery, two white onions, one or two cucumbers, and two cloves of garlic.

Chop these as finely as possible, and add the rest of the ingredients: whole-grain mustard, pepper, oregano, and salt.

Mix these together well and put them in a pot, heating them gradually, and leave on the fire ten minutes, stirring them with a wooden spoon.

Let the mince cool before filling the chiles with it.

Chiles rellenos y avinagrados
STUFFED AND VINEGARED CHILES [2]

——

Put the chiles in a tray of well-salted water and leave them for three days. At the end of this time, take them out of the salt water and cover them with boiling water, leaving them in it until the following day, when you take them out; remove the crown, the seeds, and the veins.

Let them drain, and on the side make a *picadillo* of a very fresh white cabbage, which should be chopped as finely as possible, seasoning it with salt, pepper, and whole-grain mustard. Follow all the instructions for making vinegared chiles.

Chiles avinagrados
VINEGARED CHILES

——

Select some large fresh chiles, chop them, put them in an enameled tray covered with a lot of salt, and leave them in it overnight. The next day wipe each chile with a cloth, sprinkle with peppercorns and some cloves, and put in a clay jar. After putting all the chiles in the jar, bring vinegar to a boil with a handful of salt and a sprig of tarragon, and pour over the chiles. Cover the jar with a piece of linen and place a cover over this.

These chiles should be kept in a cool place.

Cider vinegar is preferable.

Chiles verdes
GREEN CHILES

——

After you have roasted the chiles over the coals, put them in cold water to cool them. When you roast them over the stove or in the oven, they must be very hot; wrap them in a piece of damp linen. Remove the seeds and the crown without breaking them.

EJOTES · GREEN BEANS

Ejotes en pipián
GREEN BEANS IN NUT SAUCE

———

Stew the beans and thicken them with toasted and ground peanuts.

ENCHILADAS

Enchiladas de maíz a la mexicana
MEXICAN-STYLE CORN ENCHILADAS

———

Make the *nixtamal* [see recipe later in chapter—*Translator*] with five pounds of white corn and two tablespoons of lime. Boil the corn until it acquires a white color, stirring frequently so it takes on a good color.

Remove it from the fire, and rinse in several changes of water, rubbing the corn with your hands to remove the skins. Grind the *nixtamal*, adding a half pound of flour for five pounds of ground corn, a little salt, a piece of lard, and warm water.

Knead the dough until it has a good consistency. Make small balls; rest on a napkin for five minutes.

Lightly grease a *comal* [see Ingredients and Procedures section—*Translator*] or stovetop with lard and put on a tortilla; as soon as it is set, give it a turn, taking it off the moment it starts to bubble. Put the tortillas on a plate and then fry each one in a frying pan in very hot lard.

Drain the tortillas as they are removed from the oil. Then bathe them in a sauce of red chile fried in a little lard with sesame seed and oregano. Chop four onions very fine. Pour boiling water over them, rinse immediately with cold water, and drain completely.

Slice some olives in strips, Mexican sausage, [and] grated Dutch cheese or slices of fresh cheese.

As soon as you fry each tortilla, drain it and pass through the chile sauce. Set it on a plate and put on the onion, olives, sausage, and grated or sliced cheese.

Roll up the tortilla, and place each enchilada in the serving dish. When the plate is filled, cover the enchiladas with grated cheese and whole olives. Cover the enchiladas with a lid and place in the oven, and serve very hot.

There are some who prefer to fry the chile in olive oil.

Enchiladas [1]

Make a red-chile sauce, slightly thickened, seasoned with salt and oregano. Make the water tortillas [see recipe on page 67—*Translator*] without cooking them too much. When everything is ready, bathe each tortilla in the chile sauce, drain, and fry them in a frying pan with very hot fat, enough to float them.

With a kitchen fork, hold the tortilla down and fry without pricking it so that it puffs up, turning it to cook both sides. Then drain them and put them in a dish.

Repeat with all the tortillas. Have a filling ready of finely chopped onion and chopped olives, seasoned with salt and oregano. Cover a half tortilla with one or two spoonfuls of filling and some grated aged cheese. Fold over each tortilla and elegantly place it in the serving dish, repeating until the plate is full. Sprinkle the enchiladas with finely chopped onion, whole olives, and some grated cheese.

Cover the dish and put in the oven to serve it hot.

Enchiladas [2]

—

As there are people who don't know how to make Spanish tortillas, we present this easy and convenient method.

Make a dozen or so water tortillas; flatten them with a rolling pin and cut the slices with a tinned leaf mold to the size you need.

Fry each tortilla in the frying pan with a lot of hot lard, enough so they can float in it, submersing them with a kitchen fork. Turn them until they become golden on both sides, remove them, drain them well, and put them in a dish. Dip each tortilla in red-chile sauce after frying.

Place them in another dish and fill with *picadillo,* then fold each one over; place on the serving dish until it is filled and all the tortillas are prepared.

Sprinkle the enchiladas with finely chopped onion, whole olives, red-chile sauce fried in an ounce of lard, and some grated cheese. Cover the dish and put it in the oven, and serve the enchiladas hot.

Enchiladas [3]

—

The enchiladas can be filled with sliced cheese and a filling of onions and olives, pork and garlic, cumin, oregano, and chile, or with a *picadillo* of sausage prepared with olives, chopped onion, oregano, cumin, and grated cheese.

Stew the meat filling a little for these enchiladas.

ENSALADAS · SALADS

Ensalada de lechuga
LETTUCE SALAD

—

After preparing the lettuce, put it on a tray. Put the salt, pepper, a teaspoon of French mustard, [and] four tablespoons of olive oil in a soup bowl. Beat this mixture until everything is well blended, adding four or six tablespoons of vinegar. Pour the sauce over the lettuce, accompanied by sliced hard-boiled eggs, chervil, and tarragon.

Give the lettuce a few turns before putting it in the salad bowl.

Ensalada de pepinos
CUCUMBER SALAD

—

Peel the skin, then slice and put in fresh water for two hours to freshen. Remove from the water and add sliced and drained soaked onion, sliced tomatoes, two green chiles in strips, *malpica* [see Ingredients and Procedures section—*Translator*], chopped chervil, salt, pepper, and four tablespoons of oil.

Toss the salad well before adding the vinegar and oregano.

Ensalada de col
CABBAGE SALAD

—

Pick a tender cabbage and slice as finely as possible, sprinkle with salt, and let it steep several hours. Drain it well before putting [it] in the salad bowl, and add a finely chopped onion.

Next beat four egg yolks, a teaspoon of French mustard, pepper, three tablespoons of olive oil, and sufficient vinegar.

Ensalada de camarones
SHRIMP SALAD
—

First hard-boil some eggs. Separate the whites from the yolks, and mash the yolks with olive oil and a half teaspoon of French mustard.

When thoroughly mixed, add salt, pepper, and four to six tablespoons of vinegar. Separately chop some heads of lettuce until they are the right size. Finely chop the egg whites.

Mix everything with the shrimp, adding a piece of garlic and chopped chervil.

Toss the salad well, and serve on fresh lettuce leaves.

Ensalada de achicora
CHICORY SALAD
—

After cleaning the chicory, chop [it] and add very white fresh celery, cut into slices, and chervil.

Put the chicory mix in the salad bowl, splash it with salt, pepper, four or six tablespoons of olive oil, and a piece of bread rubbed with garlic.

Toss the salad well, then add three or four tablespoons of vinegar.

You can accompany the chicory salad with slices of tomato and green chile.

Ensalada de remolacha
BEET SALAD

—

Cook the beets, then peel them and slice them. Place them in a salad bowl, and sprinkle with salt, pepper, and cumin, putting on a tablespoon of olive oil and three or four of vinegar.

You can also add sliced onions to this salad, after soaking in water to tame them.

Advice: the oil and vinegar in salads vary according to taste.

Ensalada de patatas con fondos de alcachofas
POTATO SALAD WITH ARTICHOKE BOTTOMS

—

Cook the potatoes and artichokes, then carefully slice them; dress the salad with finely chopped chervil and green onion, and oil, vinegar, pepper, and salt as needed.

Ensalada de cangrejo
CRAB SALAD

—

Finely chop the crabmeat, and add some olive oil, vinegar, pepper, salt, and garlic or chopped shallots, with an equal amount of chopped lettuce.

FRIJOLES · BEANS

Frijoles rosados
PINK BEANS

———

After cooking the beans in boiling water, cover the casserole well and let them simmer on a moderate fire. Stir them from time to time and add boiling water when they dry out. Let them cook until very well done, without mashing them.

Frijoles colorados a la española
SPANISH-STYLE RED BEANS

———

Put a good piece of lard or fat in a casserole, and when it is good and hot, put in the half-drained beans and warm them.

Let them simmer for ten minutes, passing the spoon along the bottom so they don't stick. Put in a little hot water and move them to the edge of the stove where they can simmer slowly and develop flavor.

Para frijoles refritos
REFRIED BEANS

———

These are stewed with more lard and good broth. Add sliced or grated cheese when served.

Frijoles blancos guisados
STEWED WHITE BEANS

———

Put a pot on the fire with fresh lard. Fry onion, tomatoes, and green chiles. When these are half done, add the beans, not too soupy, and stew over a moderate fire.

GUISADOS · STEWS

Guisado de patatas
STEWED POTATOES

—

Peel the raw potatoes, cut them in cubes, fry them in lard, and then set them aside. Fry some onion, tomato, [and] chopped parsley, and add boiling water, salt, pepper, and oregano. Put the fried potatoes in this sauce with two or three tablespoons of grated cheese, letting them simmer over a moderate fire.

HABAS · FAVA BEANS

Habas verdes con lechuga
FRESH FAVA BEANS WITH LETTUCE

—

Cook the beans and the lettuce, then drain them.

Fry ham with garlic and finely chopped onions, then add the beans and lettuce, and simmer until the broth evaporates.

∾

Hongos o setas en tostadas
MUSHROOMS ON TOAST

—

Sauté recently harvested mushrooms, better small than large, in butter, mash with a cup of defatted broth, add a bunch of parsley and scallions, salt, pepper, and grated nutmeg, and cook over a slow fire.

Take the bundle of herbs out of the sauce, and add three egg yolks mixed with three tablespoons of good cream to it. Toast some slices of bread, moisten one side of the toast with the sauce, place them on a serving dish, and put the stewed mushrooms on the toast when serving.

∾

Niztamal
NIXTAMAL

—

Add two tablespoons of strong lime and enough water to a quart of dried corn kernels. Simmer the corn, and if the skin doesn't slip, add more lime.

After a while, the corn will start to whiten. Take it and wash it in several waters to remove the lime and the skin. Then grind the corn for dough and tortillas.

Small white corn is best for tamales.

There are new Enterprise machines for grinding corn that are excellent and are superior to all others and do more than the old Mexican *metate*. [See page 32 for a discussion of Pinedo's use of the Enterprise mill and other modern tools.—*Translator*]

Pastel de arroz a la argentina
ARGENTINE-STYLE RICE CASSEROLE

—

Cook the rice, then grind it with a spoon. To do this, move the casserole to the side of the stove. Beat the rice until it becomes like a custard, adding sugar to taste, and cinnamon.

Put a casserole on the fire with enough lard, and when very hot, pour in the rice. Fry it slowly while shaking and turning continuously. When the rice begins to dry, remove it from the fire and let [it] cool completely. Add ten beaten eggs yolks and the necessary salt.

Cover the bottom of the pan with a pastry, then put in a layer of *picadillo*, another of chicken and sauce, and cover with the rice. Moisten with syrup and cook at a slow fire until it acquires a pretty golden color.

Pastel de elote a la argentina
ARGENTINE-STYLE FRESH CORN CASSEROLE

—

Grate or grind fresh corn, then fry it in fresh lard with sugar to taste and salt.

Stir the paste constantly so it does not stick to the pan.

When the corn is cooked, but not dry, remove it from the heat and let it cool, adding ten well-beaten egg yolks, two tablespoons of butter, and a tablespoon of baking powder. Beat the paste with a wooden spoon until everything is well mixed.

Line a pie pan with the corn paste, and then add a layer of *picadillo*, another of chicken and sauce, and another of *picadillo*; cover the *picadillo* with the corn paste and baste with syrup. Bake the pie at a very low fire.

You have to watch carefully to bake the pie well.

Pastel de helote por Carmencita
LITTLE CARMEN'S CORN CAKE

—

Grate the corn, fry it in a little lard, and stir it continuously so it doesn't stick to the pan. Cook it until the corn pulls away from the casserole, without drying out too much. Continue cooking, and add ten egg yolks, two tablespoons of butter, chopped basil, sugar, salt, and a teaspoon of baking powder.

Beat the corn paste well to incorporate all the ingredients. For the *picadillo*, start by cooking a good piece of skirt steak and pork, and chop coarsely after cooking.

Grate four regular onions and six hard-cooked eggs. Cover the pie dish or tray with the corn paste, then spread a layer of the minced meat, [and] another of grated onions, eggs, pitted olives, raisins, ground oregano, cumin, and chopped basil.

Then put on a hen or some chickens, cooked and cut up in small pieces, and a spoonful of the broth the meat was cooked in. Then cover the chicken with another layer of *picadillo,* onion, eggs, olives, raisins, ground oregano, and cumin.

Pour a cup of seeded red chile over the *picadillo,* and cover everything with a layer of corn paste. Bake in the oven at a normal temperature.

Pastel caliente de legumbres
HOT VEGETABLE CASSEROLE
—

Cut carrots, turnips, potatoes, parsnips, and onions into cubes, all in equal parts. For the second part, make a *picadillo* of veal, not cooked too much.

Cover a pie dish with a rich pie pastry and on it put a layer of *picadillo,* followed by the vegetables, a cup of tomato juice with pepper, oregano, and salt, powdered with a tablespoon of flour, a cup of the broth in which the meat cooked, and some pieces of butter here and there.

Cover the pie and cook in the oven.

PATATAS · POTATOES

Patatas a la inglesa
ENGLISH-STYLE POTATOES

—

Boil in lightly salted water potatoes that have been peeled, washed, and cut in pieces, and when done, mash them with a good piece of butter and some good-quality milk.

Shape them like a pyramid on a serving dish. Pour butter on top, and then put [them] in the oven so they can take on some color.

Papas y nabos a la alemana
GERMAN-STYLE POTATOES AND TURNIPS

—

After peeling the potatoes and turnips, wash them well and put in a casserole in alternate layers, one of potatoes and one of turnips, ending with potatoes. Put in the necessary water to cook them.

Fry a tablespoon of flour, sugar, salt, and vinegar in butter. When the potatoes and turnips are done, take them out and let them drain. Mash them well and add the butter sauce.

PEPINOS · CUCUMBERS

Pepinillos avinagrados
VINEGARED CUCUMBERS

—

Carefully brush them one at a time, remove the stalk, sprinkle on some salt, and wrap them in a piece of white cloth.

Shake them strongly so that they take the salt well. Next, hang the cloth with the cucumbers in a cool place, leaving them there for several days.

After this, put them in bottles with nothing more than some raw onions. Fill the bottles with excellent cold vinegar and a half glass of brandy for each jar.

Prepared this way, the cucumbers are greener and have more flavor than those prepared with boiled vinegar.

Pepinillos encurtidos
PICKLED CUCUMBERS

Clean and crush large and small cucumbers with a rough cloth. Sprinkle them with a lot of common salt. After a while, put them in fresh water, take them out, and drain them. Then put them in a porcelain jar, adding a sufficient quantity of tarragon, peppercorns, onion, and a little garlic.

Cover with boiling vinegar, and after twenty-four hours, take them out and boil the vinegar again, repeating three times. Then cool them and cover the jar, storing [them] away from light and humidity, without touching them with your hands.

If the vinegar is not strong enough, add some more.

There are those who prefer not to soak the cucumbers in fresh water, only cleaning them with salt with a piece of cloth before putting them in the jar.

TAMALES

Tamales de dulce
SWEET TAMALES

——

Well-washed hominy is wiped dry with a clean linen or canvas cloth, then dried in the sun. Then grind and sift it. Pour on some of the lime water [see recipe for *nixtamal*, earlier—*Translator*].

Add to three pounds of corn more than three pounds of lard, and beat it all until it forms blisters.

Adding sugar to taste, try to thicken the dough. It must be mentioned here that sugar sours the *masa*.

To know if the dough is ready, make a little ball and drop it in boiling water. If it rises to the top, it is ready.

Make a filling for the tamales with cooked egg yolks, sugar, pine nuts, *acitrón*, and cinnamon.

Wash corn husks well and drain them during the morning, so they are not wet or damp.

Cook the tamales covered with corn husks in a marmite.

Tamales de elote de maíz dulce
SWEET CORN TAMALES
—

Grind or grate fresh corn, adding well-beaten egg yolks, sugar to taste, a little rich fresh milk, [and] a good piece of raw lard or butter. Beat it well, and cook it on the stove at low heat until it thickens.

For the rest, cook some stewing hens. Cut them up and remove the bones. Put the meat in a sauce made of some finely chopped onion, tomatoes, chopped, skinned, seeded green chiles, a slice of bread soaked in water and squeezed dry, salt, and pepper. After putting the chicken in the sauce, add a little oregano, and adjust the seasoning over low heat.

Now make the tamales, and cook them as usual.

For five dozen tamales, use three hens and ten dozen ears of corn.

Tamales de helote de maíz blanco o amarillo
WHITE OR YELLOW CORN TAMALES
—

For white or yellow corn tamales you do not need to put in eggs, butter, or milk.

Beat the dough with sugar and a good piece of very fresh beef lard; there is no need to put it to set like those of sweet corn.

You make the tamales like the others, with the hens and the sauce.

Tamales de carne de buey
BEEF TAMALES
—

Take a good piece of fat skirt steak and another piece of plate [see Ingredients and Procedures section—*Translator*].

Cut the meat in little half-inch pieces and put to cook in salted water. Carefully remove the scum, then cover the marmite tightly and let it simmer two hours.

Remove it from the broth and drain well.

For the next part, chop sufficient onion and fry in good fat, and when it begins to brown, add a tablespoon of flour and stir the sauce so it doesn't stick or toast the flour too much. Then add a good, thick red-chile sauce, seasoned with salt, oregano, toasted and ground red-chile seeds, and Spanish olives. Then place the meat in the sauce, letting it simmer over a long, slow fire until it is well seasoned.

If you need to add pork to the tamales, it is cooked separately and put with the beef when placed in the sauce.

The corn dough is beaten with the meat broth, adding more lard, salt, and one or two tablespoons of baking powder if you like.

You must beat the dough well before making the tamales.

Cook them like the rest, well wrapped in leaves.

Beat the dough with your hands or with a wooden spatula until it is very smooth.

Tamales de harinilla de maíz blanco
WHITE CORNMEAL TAMALES
—

Pick the first-quality and the whitest cornmeal.

The evening before making the tamales, cook a fat piece of skirt steak and a piece of salt pork. Skim the foam, and let them simmer two hours.

Remove the meat, and wet the cornmeal with the broth, putting it into a clay jar while hot.

Cover the jar and leave it until the next day. Then add more lard and salt, beating it well to make the tamales in the same way you make the beef tamales.

Tamales de gallina
STEWING-HEN TAMALES

———

Having cleaned the hens, cut in small pieces and parboil in lightly salted water, being careful to remove the foam that rises to the surface.

After the hens have cooked, take them out of the water and drain; put them in a red-chile sauce, adding two young squabs cut in very small pieces.

Follow the instructions for beef tamales.

The young squabs should be roasted when they are two weeks old.

Tamales al vapor (ultima novedad)
STEAMED TAMALES (THE LATEST THING)

———

After preparing the *nixtamal* dough as explained, take a pudding mold, greasing the inside with lard.

Next cover the interior part of the mold with a layer of the dough or paste, then put inside [it] the meat or hen stew. This should be very thick and prepared as already explained for tamales.

Then cover the stew with another layer of the same dough or paste. Having done this, cover the mold with a napkin, and over this the cover, which should be carefully adjusted so the steam doesn't enter the tamale. Put the mold in a pot of simmering water, which should come halfway up the mold. If the water evaporates, add more.

Using a small mold, the tamale should be cooked in two hours, and if large, in three.

～

Tomates conservados
PRESERVED TOMATOES

Pick red and very ripe tomatoes, peel them with boiling water, cut into quarters, and remove some of the seeds.

Next, put them on the fire in a casserole enameled on the inside. Boil them on a lively fire for fifteen minutes, without stirring them, only passing the spoon along the bottom of the pan.

When the tomatoes have finished their cooking, put them in tin cans, covering them immediately with their respective tops, and wax or lacquer [them] all around.

In the broth left from the tomatoes put two or three dozen red chiles with their crowns removed and without seeds. These you can use in fillings, stews, or sauces, storing [the chiles] like the tomatoes.

ৎ

Zanahorias tiernas con crema
YOUNG CARROTS IN CREAM

Scrape the carrots, wipe them, slice them, and cook them in water with salt. When they are half done, pour on top half a cup of good cream, then cook them on a slow fire.

A moment before serving, add three well-beaten egg yolks.

RELLENOS

STUFFINGS

Relleno blanco para aves asadas
WHITE STUFFING FOR ROAST BIRDS

Lightly boil the liver, heart, and gizzards of the poultry. Chop them as finely as possible, [and] add white bread soaked in rich milk, two tablespoons of butter, four raw eggs, six stuffed olives, a finely chopped onion, and salt. Also chop the olives.

Mix it well so [that] when you're finished, everything is well blended. If the stuffing is dry when finished, add more milk. Stuff the poultry with this mixture.

This stuffing can be served hot or cold. If you like it whiter, slice the bread thinner.

Relleno dulce
SWEET STUFFING

Add to a pound of clarified sugar, half a quart of white wine, a little salt, a quarter ounce of ground cinnamon, clove, paprika, half a pound of aged cheese, seeded raisins, almonds, two ounces of toasted sesame seed, and a little orange-blossom water. Add two egg yolks beaten without the whites, pour them into the mixture, stir, and put on the fire to cook the egg.

Separately parboil the hens in water and wine. Then stuff them with the mixture and put in the oven, basting them first with butter.

144

Relleno para ganso
STUFFING FOR GOOSE

Finely chop some cooked mushrooms, four green onions, parsley, and young garlic, all finely chopped.

Separately, chop the liver and heart of the goose. Mix and season them, adding a good piece of butter, with some lemon juice, pepper, and salt.

Relleno para pato asado
STUFFING FOR ROAST DUCK

Take the duck meat and an equal quantity of veal loin, and some raw lard in a larger quantity than the meat.

Chop finely together onions, mushrooms, parsley, and a little cream.

Stuff the ducks with this and roast them at a high temperature.

Relleno para costillas
STUFFING FOR RIBS

Finely chop a dozen shallots, a cup of mushrooms, and sufficient parsley.

Put a pot on the fire with butter and put in the shallots and mushrooms.

When they're fried, add three tablespoons of oil, two handfuls of bread crumbs, the parsley, pepper, and salt.

Relleno para lechón asado
STUFFING FOR ROAST PIG

Take the liver from the pig and remove the membrane.

Chop it a little, and grind it in a mortar with some bread crumbs moistened in cream, chicken breasts, and fresh butter, each in equal quantities with the liver, and stuffed olives.

Add sufficient chopped parsley, tarragon, some sage leaves, grated nutmeg, pepper, and salt, with two whole eggs and three yolks.

Mix it all together well, and stuff the pig, covering the stuffing with a slice of bread, and sew it shut.

Put the pig in the roasting pan and sprinkle with olive oil. The pig stuffed in this way must be cooked slowly so the stuffing is also thoroughly cooked.

Relleno para pichones asados
STUFFING FOR ROAST SQUABS

Chop some cooked mushrooms, onion, and parsley.

Mix together with a good piece of fresh butter, lemon juice, pepper, and salt.

When it's all well mixed, fill the squab or quail with this stuffing.

Relleno de patatas para aves asadas
POTATO STUFFING FOR ROAST BIRDS

Peel some raw potatoes, wash them in fresh water, and cook them.

When they are perfectly done, mash them with a potato masher. Add one-third of their weight of bread soaked in rich milk, two tablespoons of butter, half an onion, finely chopped parsley, half a ground clove of garlic, oregano, and salt.

If the stuffing is too stiff, you can add milk to make it moist.

Stuff the poultry with this dressing.

Relleno para pescado
STUFFING FOR FISH [1]

Chop crabmeat and add equal parts of white bread, moistened with milk, some cooked and chopped mushrooms, and a handful of parsley, also chopped, with salt, pepper, and grated nutmeg. Mix it all together with a good piece of butter and stuff the fish with it.

Relleno para pescados
STUFFING FOR FISH [2]

Take the fillets of two small fish, chop them, and add an equal quantity of bread crumbs moistened with fresh milk. Add to this two tablespoons of melted butter, salt, pepper, and chopped parsley.

Fill the fish with this stuffing and close the opening.

Line the dish with bacon, put in the fish, and sprinkle with flour. Then cover the fish with pieces of bacon, adding a cup of water, and cook it on a lively fire.

Whitefish is improved by stuffing.

SALSAS

—

SAUCES

ADOBOS · MARINADES

Adobo de España
MARINADE FROM SPAIN

—

Crush some garlic cloves, finely ground pepper, cloves, cinnamon, ginger, oregano, thyme, and salt. Mix in equal parts of vinegar and water.

Slice pork or lamb loins into pieces and place in a greased pot, and add enough adobo to cover the meat.

Cover, and keep the pot tightly lidded for a period of eight days without looking. Then cook the meats in the sauce until it is completely reduced and only the fat from the meat remains. Fry the meat until tender.

The marinade can be preserved for three or four months by taking the precaution of removing it from the pot only with a wooden spoon used for nothing else.

Adobo para viandas
MARINADE FOR MEATS

—

Mix the meat with sliced ham, clove, cinnamon, garlic, pepper, and chopped parsley. Put it in a marinade of white wine, vinegar, plenty of oregano, mint, thyme, bay leaf, parsley, garlic, onion, ground spices, ham slices, orange slices, and some limes. The next day take it out to cook in water and drippings or lard. Cook until all the water is gone, put it on a plate, and slice.

Otro adobo para viandas
ANOTHER MARINADE FOR MEATS

—

Grind roasted and soaked chiles with garlic cloves, oregano, cumin, ginger, bay leaf, thyme, vinegar, and salt. After making the marinade and cutting up the meat, make a layer of meat in a bowl and then one of marinade, and add some lemon slices to give it a better taste. This marinade can be used with lamb or pork.

Adobo para carne de cerdo
MARINADE FOR PORK

—

Grind soaked but unroasted chiles in a mortar with plenty of garlic.
Add a little good vinegar, more or less depending on how much you will need; then grind with oregano, mint, pepper, and salt.

Adobo de rango
CLASSY MARINADE

—

Make it with salt, vinegar, chopped savory, marjoram, garlic, wine, and all the spices.

Adobo para viandas de almendras y nueces
ALMOND-WALNUT MARINADE FOR MEATS

A marinade is made with garlic, cumin, cloves, cinnamon, and pepper, ground together and mixed with watered-down and seasoned vinegar.

Place the meats or birds that will be served with the nut sauce into the marinade to pickle and marinate overnight. The following day, cook them in the same marinade.

Grind equal quantities of cleaned and moistened walnuts and almonds with bread dipped in vinegar. When ground, fry in lard, and put the marinated birds or meat with its juice into the sauce, bringing it all to a boil until the nut sauce is thickened.

If the sauce separates, you can add a soup spoon of olive oil.

Adobo para pollos
MARINADE FOR CHICKEN

Cut the chicken in slices and place in a casserole with ground spices, wine, vinegar, almonds, *acitrón,* walnuts, and some garlic cloves.

Then put it all in a pot covered with a plate and seal with pastry all around.

Add more wine if needed while cooking.

Adobo para lomos
MARINADE FOR LOINS

Cut the loins into pieces; put in a ceramic dish with equal parts of water and vinegar, rosemary, bay leaves, clove, cinnamon, cumin, oregano, salt, and pepper. Leave in the marinade for three days, then fry them, add some broth, and leave them on the fire until the meat is almost dry.

Adobo seco
DRY MARINADE
—

Start cooking plenty of ground red chiles, adding tomatoes, garlic, and cumin.

When everything is blended, fry it in lard, and while it is on the fire add the meat so it can develop flavor together [with the adobo], adding at the same time a little vinegar. Keep it on the fire until the broth reduces so it is almost dry.

༄

Nogada para chiles rellenos
WALNUT SAUCE FOR STUFFED CHILES
—

Grind some clean walnuts, some soaked toasted ancho chile, and some toasted ground cumin. Fry the chile and cumin. Make a chile salsa, add the nuts and toasted bread, and leave it to cook until done.

When the salsa is ready, pour it over the stuffed chiles. When serving, sprinkle with some drops of olive oil.

SALSAS · SAUCES

Salsa, o el adorno de una mesa
SAUCE, OR THE ORNAMENT OF THE TABLE
—

Cut two pounds of beef in the shape of fat fingers, another [pound] of ham, two large carrots, and three onions.

Put it all in a large casserole over the fire, and add a pound of butter, the juice of three or four lemons, three cloves, a little basil, two chopped bay leaves, a little thyme, pepper, and the corresponding salt. Simmer until it has reduced by half; take it off the fire, and pour in a ceramic jar to use when you need.

Salsa española
SPANISH SAUCE

—

Put in a casserole two beef loins, a pheasant or four partridge, something like half of the [amount of] beef in ham, four or five large carrots, and five onions, one of which is stuck with five cloves.

Wet the meats with a bottle of dry Madeira and a spoonful of gelatin. Put the casserole on a large burner, and when the broth is almost gone, move it to a slow fire.

When the gelatin acquires an excellent yellow color, take it from the fire and let it cool for ten minutes, so the gelatin can easily be removed.

Salsa de nueces para todo
WALNUT SAUCE FOR EVERYTHING

—

After cleaning the walnuts, grind them with fried bread and a little ancho chile, deveined and toasted in lard to give it color.

Fry the ground mixture in oil and season it with pepper and clove, both ground, broth, and a little vinegar.

Put whatever you are serving in the sauce and let it simmer until it thickens.

Put in the salt after the sauce has simmered so it does not cause the sauce to separate.

Salsa para pescados
SAUCE FOR FISH

Put a tablespoon of lard in a pan without heating it too much, adding a bunch of parsley, scallions, green garlic, and basil, all well chopped, salt, pepper, half a cup of water, and the juice of a lemon.

Stir the sauce without stopping until it develops a good consistency. Pour the sauce on the fish at the moment it is served.

Salsa general
COMMON SAUCE

In a quart of broth, mix in a half glass of white wine, lemon slices, two bay leaves, and a little vinegar, salt, and pepper.

Let this mixture infuse on a low fire for a period of ten or twelve hours. Pass it through a sieve to serve with all kinds of poultry, vegetables, and fish.

This sauce has the advantage of keeping well for many days.

Salsa de aceitunas y almendras
OLIVE AND ALMOND SAUCE

Fry chopped garlic in lard. Then add enough tomato, toasted and grated bread, olives, chile, *acitrón*, cleaned almonds, saffron, sugar, salt, and boiling water.

Let the sauce simmer at a moderate flame for use the way you like.

Salsa para pollos
SAUCE FOR CHICKEN

—

Roast and grind tomatoes with garlic and cumin; cook the livers and gizzards of the chickens and chop them very small, putting everything together and frying it; add capers, chopped parsley, vinegar, thyme, and a little butter, [and] thicken the sauce with toasted bread and salt. Put the cooked chickens in this sauce.

Salsa a la española para pulpa de carne de buey, o sea beefsteak
SPANISH-STYLE STEAK SAUCE

—

After frying the slices of meat in the frying pan, take them out, and in the lard, which should be very scanty, fry two chopped onions, letting them brown. To these, add three tomatoes and some well-chopped green chiles, garlic, a tablespoon of butter, oregano, pepper, and salt. Let the sauce cook over a low fire until it becomes thick.

Put the slices of beef in the dish in which they will be served, covering them with the sauce and surrounding them with fried potatoes.

Salsa bechamel con setas para ostras
BECHAMEL SAUCE WITH MUSHROOMS FOR OYSTERS

—

Fry a good handful of mushrooms cut in very small pieces in a tablespoon of butter or very fresh lard, adding some young garlic cloves and a tablespoon of flour. Stir them briskly to avoid the lard taking on too much color, then add, a little at a time, two cups of milk, salt, and pepper, and let it cook until the sauce develops a good consistency.

Serve the sauce over the oysters.

Salsa para ensaladas
SALAD DRESSING
—

[Mix] two raw eggs, well beaten, a tablespoon of melted butter, four tablespoons of vinegar, and a half teaspoon of French mustard.

Beat the mixture well until it becomes a cream.

Salsa de mostaza para ensaladas
MUSTARD SALAD DRESSING
—

Take a tablespoon of French mustard and add tarragon, chervil, and garlic, all well chopped, and some tablespoons of vinegar.

Stir well until everything is perfectly mixed, then add enough olive oil.

If the sauce becomes too thick, add some vinegar, then serve in a sauce dish.

Salsa de tomate a la española
SPANISH-STYLE TOMATO SAUCE
—

Cut ten ripe tomatoes, two medium onions cut in strips, four shallots, young garlic, parsley, thyme, marjoram, peppercorns, and the necessary salt. Put these in butter with two tablespoons of Spanish sauce [see recipe on page 152—*Translator*].

After simmering the sauce well, pass the tomatoes through a sieve, using a wooden spoon to push the sauce through.

If it seems too thin, you can reduce it over a very moderate fire, but do not stop stirring so that it won't stick to the pan.

Salsa picante de chile colorado
SPICY RED-CHILE SAUCE

Remove the crowns, then flatten and devein ten or twelve chiles; toast them in a warm oven, and when they are quite toasted, take them out and put them in cold water, then hot. Wipe them off and put in a casserole.

Bathe the chiles in boiling water; let them soak for one or two hours, or let them simmer.

Then take them out of the water in which they have been soaking; add a small amount of fresh water so the sauce will have a uniform consistency.

After grinding the chiles well in a mortar, pass the sauce through a heavy strainer.

Salsa de chile verde
GREEN-CHILE SAUCE

Select some very ripe tomatoes. Peel them and remove the seeds.

For the next part, clean some green chiles and an onion. Chop each separately as finely as possible.

Mix everything together in the dish in which you will serve the sauce, adding two tablespoons of olive oil, two of vinegar, powdered oregano, and salt.

Salsa de chiles verdes para conservas
GREEN-CHILE SAUCE FOR PRESERVING
—

Select a case of very ripe tomatoes and pour boiling water over them to peel them. Cut them in quarters and remove the top part of the tomato with part of the seeds.

Put the prepared tomatoes in an enameled kettle.

To the tomatoes add half a case of green chiles, skinned, without veins or seeds, and finely chopped. Set it to cook. After the sauce has simmered and is finished, fill tin cans that are hermetically sealed to preserve the sauce well.

Another way, you can remove the crowns from the chiles, remove the seeds, wash them, and put them in with the tomatoes.

SALSAS PARA PUDINES · PUDDING SAUCES

Salsa de oro
GOLD SAUCE
—

A cup of sugar, a cup of water, a very full tablespoon of cornstarch, an egg yolk, an ounce of fresh butter, nutmeg, and sherry or Madeira wine.

Salsa para pudin
PUDDING SAUCE

———

One cup of powdered sugar, half a cup of well-mixed butter; beat them together for ten or fifteen minutes.

When the sugar is very white, add some tablespoons of whisky or sherry.

Beat the sauce well, and serve in a pyramid-shaped crystal dish.

Salsa de frutas conservadas
PRESERVED FRUIT SAUCE

———

Make a batter of sugar and butter, beating the mixture with a fork for a period of ten or fifteen minutes, or until the batter has been converted into a white cream.

When everything is well mixed, add half a glass of the liquid from the preserved fruits used in making the pudding [for which the sauce is intended].

If the pudding was made with fresh fruits, in place of the liquid substitute a half glass of brandy or wine in the batter.

Salsa transparente para pudines o pasteles
CLEAR SAUCE FOR PUDDINGS OR CAKES

———

Dissolve two or three tablespoons of corn flour in cold water and put the liquid in boiling water, adding a good piece of fresh butter and juice of the fruits that were used in the pudding or cakes.

If the fruits were preserved, add a cup of the liquid passed through a sieve, or juice of lemon, orange, or pineapple.

DULCES

—

Agua de anis
ANISE WATER

—

Take four ounces of cleaned anise and infuse it for a month in two *azumbres* of brandy; clarify it and add a pound and a half of sugar dissolved in an *azumbre* of water; mix it well and filter it.

Note: an *azumbre* equals a half gallon.

∾

Almendras sopladas
ALMOND PUFFS

—

Finely chop a pound of almonds, then add them to egg whites and twelve ounces of powdered sugar, beat them to snowy peaks, then spread them on sheets of white paper and put them in the oven.

∾

Arroz en leche de almendras
RICE IN ALMOND MILK

—

Take a proportional quantity of clean almonds, grind them, and put them in the milk, then pass it through a sieve several times.

Then add two tablespoons of rice flour and the right amount of sugar; put everything in a pot, and while it is on the fire stir it constantly so it does not stick to the pot.

When it thickens like blancmange, pour it in the serving dish and sprinkle with cinnamon and sugar.

While this is clearer, it is better to make cornmeal gruel for the ill.

∾

Barquillos de moda
STYLISH CONES
—

A quart of sifted flour, half [a] cup of yeast, a teaspoon of salt, six well-beaten eggs, two tablespoons of powdered sugar, and two tablespoons of butter.

Beat everything well, and thin the batter with warm milk to the consistency of a frying batter.

Put the bowl in a quiet place to rise for two hours.

Grease the mold with lard, making sure not to miss the deep corners on the inside. Next put the batter in the mold and close it. When the cones are cooked on one side, turn the mold over to cook them on the other. When they have browned and taken on a pretty color, take the cones from the mold.

These are good very hot, just taken from the mold, served well powdered with sugar.

You can add different kinds of extracts to the batter, and two tablespoons of brandy. You can also make them with baking powder.

∾

Bizchochos de chocolate
CHOCOLATE BISCUITS

———

Beat or stir well in a mortar six fresh eggs; add an ounce of finely powdered chocolate and four ounces of finely ground sugar. Crush everything in the mortar until it becomes paste, and put it in papers or molds.

Bizchochos de maíz
CORN BISCUITS

———

Beat six egg whites with an ounce of sugar; when they become very foamy, mix in six beaten yolks, then add cornmeal and an ounce of melted butter. Knead well, adding cornmeal to give the dough a normal biscuit texture.

Put them in the molds and bake in the oven.

Bizchochos de naranja, azahar, y anis
ORANGE, ORANGE-BLOSSOM WATER, AND ANISE BISCUITS

———

Beat fifteen egg whites with a pound of finely ground sugar, and when they are whipped, add the yolks, beaten until they are very thick.

Then add three soup cups of yeast and the juice of half an orange with a half pound of melted butter; put in a little anise and a quart of orange-blossom water or milk.

Stir it very well, and add as much flour as it will absorb, so the dough has a consistency that is not too stiff and not too loose.

Make the biscuits and leave them until they have risen, then put them in the oven when it reaches a moderate temperature.

∾

Bocadillos del Cónsul
THE CONSUL'S SNACK

—

Make a syrup with a pound of sugar, clarified a little higher than *panocha* [see Ingredients and Procedures section—*Translator*]; add a grated coconut, a half pound of skinned and ground almonds, and a quart of custard.

Put it on the fire to simmer a little, and take it off to cool. Once cool, add fourteen beaten egg yolks. Put it on the fire again until it simmers, being careful to stir it well and without stopping until it thickens, then pour it on the platter.

CAFÉ · COFFEE

Café
COFFEE [1]

—

There are many ways of making coffee, and here we employ the easiest way to make it perfectly, without losing the aroma.

Put two cups of coffee in a coffee pot, pour on boiling water, and stir the coffee with a spoon without stopping so it does not rise and spill; remove the coffee from the fire for a moment, and add a half cup of fresh water. Put the coffee pot on the edge of the stove for the coffee to steep for ten minutes, without boiling, as this is how it loses all its merit.

Café
COFFEE [2]

———

Put a cup of coffee in a soup cup with the yolk of a fresh egg: stir the coffee with a spoon so it mixes well: cover the cup and leave it five minutes: then put the coffee in a coffee pot and pour on boiling water, leaving it to steep at the edge of the stove, without allowing it to boil.

∾

Cajeta de camote blanco
WHITE-YAM CARAMEL

———

Add a pound of ground white yam, a half pound of ground almonds, and half a coconut to three pounds of sugar or clarified medium-thick syrup.

Put it all on the fire, and when it turns to caramel, add a half quart of cream, or more if necessary. When it thickens to the point of falling off the ladle, remove it from the fire and fill the box.[1]

Cajeta de leche y piña
MILK AND PINEAPPLE CARAMEL

———

Add a soup cup of pineapple juice to eight quarts of milk, four pounds of sugar, and six ounces of cornstarch.

Put this on the fire to boil, and let it cook until it comes to the caramel stage.

∾

———

1. The box (a *cajeta* is a small box) is the mold in which the candy jells.— *Translator*

Capirotada, o pudin a la española
SPANISH-STYLE PUDDING
—

Slice the bread thinly and toast it in the oven until it becomes a beautiful brown color.

Slice some smooth white cheese. Test some on the stove; if it makes threads, it is good.

Hard-boil eight eggs and slice them. Melt a piece of butter in a casserole, and when hot, add two chopped green onions or half a regular onion, two tablespoons of tomatoes, and salt.

When finished, without letting the sauce get too dry, add some boiling water, a small cup of raisins, pepper, and some sugar, as the sauce should be quite sweet. Let it simmer while the flavor develops, then spread it over the bottom of a flat serving dish that can take the oven heat. Place a layer of bread on the bottom of the dish, another of cheese, and another of sliced eggs. Baste both layers with a layer of the sauce, distributing the onions and the raisins. Add another layer of bread, cheese, and eggs, moistening these with the sauce and adding raisins. Finish the last layer with bread, and cover with the sauce, raisins, and onions.

Put the dish on the side of the stove to heat, without bringing it to a boil. When it is very hot, put [it] in the oven on some tiles to brown, without boiling it.

Serve it very hot. You can also add to the layers almonds or [other] cleaned chopped nuts.

∾

Caramelos de limón
LEMON CARAMELS
—

A pound of ground sugar, half a cup of water, an ounce of butter, an egg, [and] four drops of lemon oil. Put everything together, bring it to a boil, then test them in a little water; if they drop in the water and harden, they are ready.

Do not stir the mixture while boiling, but give it two turns when you put in the lemon oil. Then pour it in a pan greased with butter on the inside. Mark them when they are cool, and cut them into squares. Wrap them in wax paper.

CHOCOLATE

Chocolate en agua
CHOCOLATE IN WATER
—

Put the tablet [of chocolate] with water on the fire, in an amount a little larger than you need to fill the chocolate cup you are going to serve it in, and when you have brought it to a boil, take it off and completely break up the tablet with the chocolate beater, and mix it with the water.

Put it back on the fire to boil, and when it starts to rise, remove it a second time. To serve, beat it and pour half a cup, and return to beating. Then fill the cup, making sure the top is covered with foam.

Chocolate con leche
CHOCOLATE MILK

Place a bar of chocolate in water over the fire, and when it starts to boil, remove the pot from the heat. Dissolve the chocolate completely. Whip it with the chocolate beater and return to the fire. Add enough boiled milk to fill the chocolate cups in which it will be served. Vigorously beat the chocolate mixture to incorporate it with the milk. Return it to the fire and bring it to a boil again, then remove it from the heat and beat it if you want it to foam.

Next, beat some separated egg whites and yolks. When the whites are very stiff, add the yolks, which should be well beaten. Put them in the chocolate cups with a chocolate beater or a whisk.

Add the chocolate a little at a time, continuously beating it until the chocolate cups are full.

To serve, half fill a cup and beat it vigorously. Then fill the cup, making sure the top is covered with foam.

∾

Coco de boda
WEDDING COCONUT

Add two grated or ground coconuts to three pounds of clarified sugar of a medium density, put it all together, and give it a little boil. After taking it off the fire and letting it cool, add ten egg yolks, half a bottle of white wine, and a little orange-blossom water. Return it to the fire until it becomes as thick as dough.

Then put it on a tray and brown it.

CONSERVAS · PRESERVES

Conserva de sandia (la reina de Cuba)
WATERMELON PRESERVE (THE QUEEN OF CUBA)

—

Select a good watermelon; slice it, and remove all the green skin with the point of a knife, then boil the slices several times until they are half cooked. Separate them and put in cool water. Change the water several times until it has lost the bad flavor and then put the slices in a clarified syrup, leaving them so that they preserve until they become transparent.

This conserve is prepared by boiling [it] in water with salt.

Also for the fig conserve [see page 168—*Translator*], give them a light boiling in salted water.

Confites de naranja
CANDIED ORANGE

—

Select the most beautiful oranges. Remove the yellow rinds lightly with a knife, and divide into quarters.

Remove the seeds, and carefully put the oranges in cold water, and [then] braise them in boiling water, leaving them no longer than necessary to prepare them. Remove them to some cold water, and when they are soft and tender, take them out and put them in a heavy syrup. After several boilings, remove from the fire and let cool again.

Remove the oranges from the syrup and put them in jelly jars, pouring over the top the syrup, which you have boiled a little longer after removing the oranges. Let [the syrup] cool before adding it to the jelly jars.

Conserva de naranja dulce
SWEET ORANGE PRESERVE

—

Select the largest Chinese oranges, and cut off the colored surface of their skins with the cells of the essential oil, leaving the white part and the veins.

Make a hole in the crown, and through this pierce the sections with a thin knife, leaving the juice that was not squeezed out.

Cook them, remove them from the fire, let them cool, and squeeze them without bruising them. Put them in clean water, which you change several times a day, until they have lost all their bitterness.

Then put them in a syrup thick enough so they reach the state of conserve over a mild fire, repeating this operation for three consecutive days. On the third, add some water to the syrup and let it boil until they equally reach the point of high conserve. Remove the seeds and cover it well.

Conserva de higos verdes
GREEN FIG PRESERVE

—

Make an incision in one side of the green figs, from the stem to the flower. This allows the best penetration of the syrup.

Let them soak overnight in some well-settled lime water.

The next day rinse them in several changes of water, and then boil them in salted water. Then peel them and put them in fresh water, changing it several times. Put them in clarified syrup, with five pounds of figs for six pounds of sugar, and boil for two hours. Remove from the fire, and the next day return them to the boil until they have reached the right consistency for a preserve.

Conserva de calabaza
SQUASH PRESERVE

—

Cut the squash in pieces and remove the skin and seeds. Put it in slaked lime water for several hours. Take out the squash and wash it well in several waters.

Put it in a cold and thin clarified syrup. Keep it over a gentle fire, being advised that each medium squash requires three pounds of sugar in syrup.

Conserva de membrillo
QUINCE PRESERVE

—

Select about eight ripe and good-sized quinces and cut them in pieces, making four to six quarters from each.

Carefully remove the heart from them, and put in fresh water to soak.

Next put the quinces in a marmite or pot, with enough medium-thick clarified syrup, and let them cook until the syrup thickens well, then add some anise as you've been told.

∾

Crema de almendras
ALMOND CREAM

—

Crush six sweet almonds and two bitter almonds, put them in a quart of milk, and add a tablespoon of orange water, two ounces of sugar, and two egg yolks.

Put it all to cook, stirring and triturating everything while it cooks. When the cream is done, remove it from the fire and pass it through a sieve, and cool in the dish in which it will be served.

Crema de vino
WINE CREAM

—

Beat eight egg yolks in a sufficient quantity of powdered sugar, then add a bottle of Malaga wine a little at a time and triturate it constantly. Put it on the fire and beat it constantly until the cream is perfectly blended with the wine.

HELADOS · ICES

Helados de albericoque
APRICOT SHERBET

—

Soak the apricots, which should be very ripe. Remove the pits and pass three pounds of the fruit through a sieve, adding a quart of cooked sugar syrup to the paste.

For the next part, grind a dozen cleaned apricot kernels, letting them infuse for an hour in the juice of two lemons with a few spoonfuls of fresh water.

Pass the kernels through a sieve and add the juice to the apricots. Freeze it in this state.

Helados de piña y naranja
PINEAPPLE-ORANGE SHERBET

—

After picking the oranges, remove the skin and make pieces while removing the seeds: mash them and pass them through a sieve. Take twenty ounces of orange juice [and] eight ounces of sugar made into a syrup in a quart of water. Add some vanilla extract and put it all in the ice-cream freezer to make the ice.

Helados de tuberosas
TUBEROSE ICE
—

Put an ounce of tuberoses in a vase, having removed the leaves of the plant. Pour six quarts of water on top, in which you have already dissolved twelve ounces of sugar over the fire, but so that it is only lukewarm, without letting it boil or get too warm. Leave the flowers in the infusion for four hours, stirring the vase from time to time. Then pass the mixture through a very fine linen and put it in the ice-cream freezer to make the ice.

Helados por la señorita Angelina
MISS ANGELINA'S ICE CREAM
—

Put three quarts of very fresh milk to boil; when the milk has boiled well, add four or five ounces of cornstarch dissolved in a little cold milk.

Stir the milk well to avoid coagulation when mixing in the cornstarch.

As soon as the cream thickens, remove it from the fire without letting it boil, and allow it to cool.

Then beat nine eggs, separating the whites from the yolks, beating the whites until they form peaks; to the yolks add two small cups of granulated sugar, and beat them well before mixing with the whites, beating them both before adding to the cool cream.

Perfume this to taste.

Empty the cream into the ice-cream maker to set. This is enough to make a gallon of ice cream.

∿

Horchata catalan
CATALAN ORGEAT

—

Beat eight egg yolks, and heat [this] slowly at the beginning so it doesn't set. Take the liquid off the fire, then beat in a quart of Catalan brandy or good Californian brandy.

After sweetening to taste, add a little powdered cinnamon, with some lemon water and half a pound of ground almonds, letting them settle. You can make any quantity you wish.

JALEAS · JELLIES

Jalea de naranjas
ORANGE JELLY

—

Pass the orange juice through a silk sieve and let it rest; filter, clarify it, and pass it through again before mixing it with the rind of an orange.

Add some perfectly clear syrup to thicken the juice; use a pound of sugar for each quart of juice, and a little gelatin. To test if the jelly is ready, put a spoon of jelly in very cold water; if it falls to the bottom of the glass and jells, it is ready.

Jalea de grosella
RED-CURRANT JELLY

—

[Take] four quarts of seeded red currants, not too ripe, a quart of raspberries, and five quarts of white sugar.

Layer the currants with sugar and keep the raspberries separate, well covered with sugar.

Both fruits need to macerate with the sugar for five hours.

Then put the mixture on the fire, stirring it with a wooden spatula and taking care that the jelly heats a little at a time.

When it has all come to a boil, put some drops of the jelly in a spoon, then put this in fresh water; if the jelly is cooked enough, it will jell on the spoon when cool.

When it gets to this point, put in the raspberries with the sugar in the pot and let it boil a few minutes at the end to add aroma to the jelly. Then pass it through a sieve without pressing it, and when no more liquid passes through, put the jelly in jars and let it cool.

Jalea de frambuesa y limón
RASPBERRY AND LEMON JELLY

—

Select very ripe strawberries and remove the stems, then wash them in cold water.

Thoroughly crush five pounds of strawberries and three of raspberries and add the juice of four lemons, passing [this] through a cloth before pouring into a clear syrup like the other jellies.

All the jellies are made the same. To all the jellies you can add raspberries to give them a good aroma.

Advice: when making jelly, let it boil strongly without interruption so it will turn out well.

JARABE · SYRUP

Jarabe de zumo de limón
LEMON SYRUP

———

Make a clear syrup with three pounds of sugar, and when it starts to thicken, add a quart of juice from very ripe lemons.

Let it finish boiling, take it off the heat, let it cool, and put [it] in bottles.

Jarabe de mora
BLACKBERRY SYRUP

———

Squeeze some very black blackberries, slightly before they are perfectly ripe, and put twenty-four ounces of juice in thick syrup, made with a pound of sugar. Let it all boil together for a few minutes: take it off the fire, let cool, and put [it] in dry bottles covered well.

Advice: to know if the syrup is ready, let a drop fall on a plate; if the liquid that falls scatters into many drops, you need to cook it longer, until the drop that you pour on the plate does not scatter. This is the test for knowing when you have reached the right point.

Jarabe o crema de frambuesas
RASPBERRY SYRUP OR CREAM

———

To two quarts of good brandy add half a quart of raspberry syrup made like blackberry syrup.

Jarabe de horchata a la española
SPANISH-STYLE ALMOND SYRUP

—

Take a pound of sweet almonds, two pounds of sugar, four ounces of bitter almonds, a half gallon of water, two ounces of orange-blossom water, and the rind of a lemon.

Leave the almonds in cold water long enough so that they can be easily peeled; don't use hot water as you usually do. Crush the almonds in a mortar, from time to time adding a little water and the lemon rind.

Make a paste, and dissolve with half the water, squeezing it strongly through a thick napkin, return the paste to the mortar, add water, and squeeze it again.

After this, bring some water in a pan to a boil and pour in the almond milk, stirring it until it has boiled for a few minutes.

Next, remove it from the fire and let it cool, add the orange-blossom water, and pass everything through a napkin.

Fill the bottles with this syrup, checking them from time to time, because the almond oil floats, since it is very light, and tends to separate into two parts, and the syrup can change if you do not take the precaution of shaking it to keep the syrup properly emulsified.

JIRICAYA · CUSTARD

Jiricaya commun
COMMON CUSTARD

———

Sweeten the milk to taste and simmer it with some strips of cinnamon; when it has taken on some consistency, remove it from the fire and stir it well so it doesn't form a skin.

Add egg yolks, one for each half quart of milk, and when they are well blended, put the mixture in a bowl or the cups in which it will be served. Put these in a pan with boiling water, letting the water come only halfway up the cups.

Jiricaya de nuez
WALNUT CUSTARD

———

Sweeten two soup cups of milk and add eight egg yolks and fifteen large well-ground walnuts. Strain it all, and cook the cream.

∾

Leche de almendras
ALMOND MILK

———

Stir ground and sifted rice, ground almonds, egg yolks, and sugar to taste with milk.

Put it all to cook, and before it sets, add a little orange-blossom water.

You need a quart of milk, ten egg yolks, and a handful of flour dissolved in water.

∾

Licor de naranja
ORANGE LIQUEUR
—

This product results from the fermentation of orange juice and is a pleasant wine to taste, a little alcoholic, without the flavor of the fruit it is made from, and in time takes on a taste very similar to that of dry wines.

Although there are various formulas employed by the manufacturers for the preparation of this drink, they all seem identical, but they each vary with the addition of some substances that determine the flavor. Here we give a procedure that yields the best results for the most beautiful liqueur you can obtain.

Select the cleanest and ripest fruits, peel them perfectly, and after you have removed the rinds, put them in baskets that you put on top of each other, subjecting them to a strong pressure with the aim of obtaining all the juice of the oranges.

As the juice that you get this way results in a mixture containing extraneous matter, you have to strain it through fine linen and check the operation; [then] put it in a barrel in which you already have put sugar in proportion of 18 to 20 pounds for each 150 quarts of juice, beating the mixture until the liquid and the sugar are perfectly blended. This quantity of sugar varies according to the higher or lower level of alcohol you wish to obtain.

The fermentation is then spontaneous, and when checking this operation you must be careful that the barrel is always full because the foam that is produced trickles out.

Eight days after starting, the liquid should be fermented. Decant it into another barrel, which should be perfectly clean; after a few days, when you think the secondary fermentation is enough, suspend it, pouring in a little brandy. Let the liqueur rest about a month, and then transfer it to another container in which it will stay for seven or eight months, completely covered, until the liqueur is perfectly formed. Every time you change the receptacle for the wine, you must filter it to obtain a wine entirely clear and transparent.

Also, you must observe that during the entire time you are making the liqueur you have to keep the temperature of the room no lower than twenty degrees centigrade. After the time indicated above, you can bottle it for sale.

There are several manufacturers who add a little caramel, to make the wine a notable amber color, and some add orange peels, to obtain a more pronounced flavor.

MAMONES · CAKES

Mamones de almidon
CORN FLOUR CAKES

—

Beat twenty-four eggs, separating the whites from the yolks, until they are solid.

Separately mix two small piles of powdered sugar with the whites, and when they are well blended, add the yolks, stirring everything near the stove; add to the batter eighteen ounces of corn flour, beating all the while so the flour does not form lumps. When it is all mixed, put it quickly into the pans, which should be half filled, and cook in a slow oven.

Mamones de anis
ANISE CAKES
———

Beat the separated whites and yolks of eleven eggs until they stiffen, and then mix them together. Mix them with a pound of sifted sugar and beat them until the batter is thick and white.

Then add ten ounces of corn flour and a little anise, stirring the batter to mix in the flour.

Empty the mixture into small cake molds. When they are full, put them in the oven to bake.

They can be served in slices, or you can cover them with chocolate icing and warm them in the oven a few minutes.

MERMELADAS · MARMALADES

Mermelada superior de membrillo
BEST QUINCE MARMALADE
———

Divide the quince in quarters and remove the cores; put them to cook with the skins in water. When they are well cooked, pass them through a colander or a sieve and weigh [them].

Separately cook the cores in a little water, and mix a little of the quince with the resulting jelly. Make a syrup with sugar in the proportion of a pound and a half for each pound of quince, and weigh this. Clarify it and let it cook until it sets perfectly, then remove it quickly from the fire so it does not continue boiling.

Next, while one [person] is pouring in the syrup, another is beating to keep it from burning or making balls; after having put in all the quince, continue beating until the jelly seems heavy.

It is necessary to take care that the beating is done constantly in the same direction, because if you vary the direction, it cuts the marmalade and it will not set.

Mermelada de peras y manzanas
PEAR AND APPLE MARMALADE

Take very ripe pears and apples. Peel them, and cut into small pieces, having beforehand removed the cores and seeds.

Add a soft-ball syrup, and cook until it no longer sticks to the pan. When making cakes, sprinkle with a little cinnamon.

Mermelada de mora y frambuesas
BLACKBERRY AND STRAWBERRY MARMALADE

Wash the blackberries well, and start to boil them, adding one or two pounds of strawberries. When the juice has been released, remove it from the fire, keeping the blackberries, and adding a highly clarified syrup.

This marmalade is put in hot tin cans, and sealed hermetically.

The juice the blackberries produce can be passed through a sieve to make jelly, or put with some juice with sugar or syrup.

Mermelada de uva
GRAPE MARMALADE

Take muscat grapes, very ripe and pink; remove the skin and seeds. Cook a pound of fruit and another of sugar with the juice of an orange. When it is very thick, remove from the fire, let cool, and put in jars.

Mermelada de tomate
TOMATO MARMALADE

—

Take an ounce of sugar for each large tomato and let cook until cara-melized in the kettle. Take a tenth portion of onions cut in small pieces, and when they start to color, put them on the tomatoes with salt, pep-per, clove, and nutmeg.

Mermelada de peras y higos
PEAR AND FIG MARMALADE

—

Take some autumn pears; peel them, and divide into small pieces, tak-ing out the core with the seeds.

Add a light syrup. After boiling them for two hours over a low fire, add a pound of very ripe figs for two or three pounds of pears, and let the marmalade cook until it separates from the pan.

Mermelada de albericoques
APRICOT MARMALADE

—

Select large and very ripe apricots. Peel them and cut each in four pieces, removing the stone. Put [them] in a pan with sugar, alternat-ing layers of apricots and sugar until you have filled the pan. Cover and leave without touching them for twelve hours.

Next, put the pan on the fire after adding some almonds from the same fruit, and let the marmalade cook on a low fire, taking care to continually stir it with a wooden spoon so it doesn't stick to the bot-tom of the pan.

It is good to cook it for three or four hours. Usually you need a pound of sugar for two of fruit. If the marmalade is passed through a sieve, you do not need to peel the fruit. Prepared this way, it is very pleasing and stores well.

∾

Natas reales
ROYAL CREAM

—

Bring a quart of milk to a boil, [and add] sixteen egg yolks, a cup of ground rice, and sugar to taste. When it begins to thicken, add a quart of cream and serve with powdered cinnamon.

PASTELES · CAKES

Pastel de limón o grosella
LEMON OR RED-CURRANT PIE

—

Cover the tart pans with a layer of puff pastry and edge with a wide ring of pastry. Put the tarts in the oven, and before the pastry has completely cooked, fill them with the following mixture:

Two and a half cups of boiling water, four tablespoons of butter, two cups of sugar, six full tablespoons of cornstarch, the juice of three very fresh lemons or six tablespoons of red-currant juice, [and] six yolks and three egg whites, beating the whites separately from the yolks. When the whites are snowy, add the yolks and beat them together.

When the mixture is beaten well, fill the shells and return [them] to the oven. After baking, cover the surface with egg whites, stiffly beaten with some tablespoons of powdered sugar. Put the pies in the oven for a few moments to brown the egg whites.

This quantity is for three pies.

∾

Pastillas
PASTILLES

—

All pastilles are prepared in the same way. You use a big spoon with a long point; put the spoon in the boiling syrup, to which you have added all the powdered sugar it can absorb without becoming runny. Do not stop stirring. You then drip it, drop by drop, from the point of the spoon onto sheets of white paper. This way you form larger or smaller pastilles.

To unstick them, lightly moisten the reverse side of the sheet of paper and let the pastilles dry in fresh air.

For the pastilles to have a fruit flavor, it is just a matter of using the corresponding syrup of orange, blackberry, lemon, and so on.

∾

Pililas
SOPAPILLAS

—

Make the dough with a quart of sifted flour, a spoonful of salt, and two teaspoons of baking powder. Dampen the flour with milk until it makes a smooth dough; knead it and stretch it with a rolling pin on a table sprinkled with flour, finishing the dough at the right thickness. Cut the sopapillas with a knife, in squares of a size that you like.

Next, fry them in good hot lard in a frying pan, and put some of the lard on top of the sopapillas. Give them a turn so they brown on both sides. Drain them well, and serve them very hot.

PONCHES · PUNCHES

Ponche a la española
SPANISH-STYLE PUNCH

———

Beat eight fresh egg yolks in a pitcher with a half cup of sugar. Beat the yolks for ten minutes, then add the eight egg whites, which have been beaten into stiff peaks, and sprinkle with grated nutmeg.

Slowly add a half cup of warm milk to the mixture, then a quart of very hot milk, a little at a time, beating constantly. Then add a dose of good, strong brandy.

If the punch becomes too thick, add more hot milk.

This punch can also be made with water.

If the punch is made for the sick, don't use the egg whites.

Ponche de vino tinto
RED-WINE PUNCH

———

Soak in two quarts of old wine for twenty-four hours some strips of cinnamon sticks, two whole cloves, two sour oranges, and the peel of another.

Strain the wine into a pan over slow heat, and add sugar to taste. As soon as the wine reaches the boiling point, serve in a mug.

Wine punch is served very hot.

Ponche de rón o whisky escocés
RUM OR SCOTCH-WHISKEY PUNCH

———

Put the juice of two lemons in a pan with the rind of one cut in pieces, half a quart of sugar syrup, a quart of brandy, and a half quart of rum.

Mix the sugar and liquor well. Place the pan over the fire and warm the punch moderately without bringing it to a boil.

Serve the punch very hot. If you wish, flame the vapor of the punch when it is on the table, just when it is time to serve it.

PUDINES · PUDDINGS

Pudin de arróz
RICE PUDDING

—

Put a half pound of well-washed rice to cook in two quarts of rich milk. When the rice is half done, add a piece of butter, well-washed raisins, and sugar.

Let the rice simmer on a low flame for three hours, not letting it stick to the bottom. Gently stir the rice.

When the rice is thoroughly cooked, pour it into a dish to cool, then add eight well-beaten egg yolks and four whites beaten to snowy peaks, a spoonful of lemon-blossom water, and ground cinnamon.

Pudin de señoritas
YOUNG LADIES' PUDDING

—

Clean a pound of almonds soaked in cold water and grind them in a marble mortar with a pound of sugar, sprinkling with orange-blossom water.

Beat seven eggs, and mix them with the sugar and almonds.

When finished, butter the inside of a pan and pour in the batter before baking in the oven.

Pudin de Diana
DIANA'S PUDDING
—

Toast bread to a golden color and cover with rich milk.

Beat four eggs, separating the whites from the yolks, mix them together, and add two tablespoons of sugar and two of cream. Mix it all together with the bread, adding two tablespoons of fresh melted butter, two tablespoons of baking powder, a cup of seeded raisins, two tablespoons of brandy, and cleaned almonds cut in slivers. Cook the pudding in the oven or over steam.

Serve the pudding with a butter sauce.

Pudin de naranja
ORANGE PUDDING
—

Boil three quarts of milk with a half pound of sugar and a little cinnamon. While the milk cools, stir in three ounces of butter, six egg yolks, raisins, almonds, a crumbled biscuit cake, and the rind of a mandarin orange.

Butter a dish well to hold the pudding, and bake it in the oven.

Pudin de frutas
FRUIT PUDDING
—

A pound of sifted flour, salt, a little water, four eggs, half a pound of butter, and baking powder.

Moisten the dough enough so that it will be a little firm, knead it, and stretch [it] over a napkin spread with butter; put fifty plums in the center with half a pound of well-ground raw brown sugar, cinnamon, and lemon rind. Wrap the dough in the form of a ball or lump, and lace it up with a thread as tightly as you can so it doesn't let in the water.

The pudding can be made with all types of fruit.

Pudin de Carmencita
LITTLE CARMEN'S PUDDING
—

Crumble cold cake or pound cake, sugar to taste, almonds, finely chopped *acitrón,* and ground cinnamon into a quart of milk.

Add ten whites and yolks beaten separately (the whites should be very full when they are added), and a small piece of butter.

Then grease a pan on the inside with butter, pour in the pudding, and let it cook in the oven at a low fire.

Pudin de Julieta
JULIETA'S PUDDING
—

Moisten bread or dry cake in two quarts of milk, beat, and add six well-beaten eggs, sugar, and a tablespoon of butter.

Grease the inside of a pan with butter before pouring in the batter and putting it in the oven.

When it is almost done, beat an egg white until foamy, add a tablespoon of powdered sugar, and continue beating. Cover the pudding with this, sprinkle some sugar on top, and return to the oven to brown.

Pudin de Leticia
LETICIA'S PUDDING
—

Take a quart of fresh cream, half a quart of milk, and eight egg yolks beaten well, and put to boil.

Grease a platter with butter, and put in slices of sponge cake moistened with boiling milk, and in this way make layers, one of cake and one of milk and ground cinnamon.

Be advised that the last layer should be of cream custard. Then put the platter in the oven to set.

Pudin de Rosita
ROSITA'S PUDDING
—

Take about four apples, remove the peels and core them, and chop them not too finely.

Beat separately six eggs, the whites apart from the yolks.

Then mix a good piece of butter with the apples, then put in some raisins, sugar, lemon extract, and a teaspoon of powdered cinnamon.

On the side, have enough dry bread ready that has been soaked in rich milk.

Grease a pan with butter on the inside and put in a layer of bread and a layer of apples.

Take care that the last layer is of bread.

When the pudding is almost finished, put portions of the beaten eggs here and there, on which you put a little piece of jelly.

With this effect, you can present some cakes or puddings very elegantly.

Pudin de Chonita
CHONITA'S PUDDING
—

Beat four egg yolks with four tablespoons of cornstarch and a little water. When the mixture is beaten smooth, add a small cup of milk. Pass it through a strainer, and add it to a half quart of boiling milk. If it becomes too thick, add more milk until it has the consistency of caramel, letting it simmer for fifteen minutes at low heat.

Stir it from the bottom of the pot from time to time so it doesn't stick.

Take the cream from the fire, adding two egg whites that have been well beaten with two tablespoons of powdered sugar and a pinch of salt. These should be added slowly to the cream while stirring constantly.

Put the pudding in a serving dish, sprinkling with cinnamon and lump sugar, which should be browned with a red-hot iron.

Then beat two egg whites until they make a very thick foam and add two tablespoons of powdered sugar.

Cover the pudding with this and brown in the oven until golden. It can also be served without browning the sugar, accompanied by jelly.

Pudin de pan por la señora W. Fitts
MRS. W. FITTS'S BREAD PUDDING
—

Moisten the bread in a little milk, more or less according to the amount needed for the pudding. Add four egg yolks, half a teaspoon of salt, and two tablespoons of sugar. Mix everything well. Add six peeled and sliced peaches to the mixture.

For the next layer, beat a half cup of sugar with a tablespoon of butter, and when the batter is very white, add the four egg whites and beat to stiff peaks, adding half a small cup of flour, a teaspoon of baking powder, and half a teaspoon of salt. Mix these together to make a batter.

Then take an agate baking pan, not too deep, put in the prepared bread, and cover with the batter.[2]

This pudding should be cooked in a regular oven and served with a butter sauce with wine or brandy.

If the fruits you use were preserved, take the liquid to make a clear sauce.

You can make this pudding with all fruits.

Ratafia de frutas
FRUIT RATAFIA[3]

Take two pounds of selected ripe cherries, three pounds of sour cherries, another three pounds of red currants, and three more of raspberries. Remove the stems and pits from the first, and clean the others.

Crush them all together and let rest for several hours.

Pass the juice through a napkin, add a half gallon or an *azumbre* of brandy and four ounces of sugar for each *azumbre* (half gallon) of liquor you use [see Ingredients and Procedures section—*Translator*]. Put it all in a vessel, and at the end of a month pass it through a sieve and bottle it.

2. An agate pan is an enameled metal pan. The enameling resembles the pattern of agate.—*Translator*

3. Ratafias are fruit-flavored liquors.—*Translator*

Torrejas de Olimpia
OLYMPIAN TOAST

———

Take a cup of flour, four well-beaten egg yolks, and a little warm milk. Beat the mixture well, until smooth, adding warm water to give it a uniform consistency, and then pass it through a colander. Slice slightly dry bread, then soak in sherry wine. Bathe the slices, which should be thin, in the batter and then fry them.

Make a slightly thick syrup with a little powdered cinnamon.

Put the toasts in a serving dish and cover them with the syrup.

These should be served very hot.

INGREDIENTS AND PROCEDURES

acitrón   Also known as *cubiertos de biznaga,* this is the candied fruit of the barrel cactus (*Echinocactus grandis*). To prepare it, a barrel cactus is harvested and skinned and its spines removed; then the pieces are soaked in a brine solution until firm. After this, they are boiled with sugar until crystallized.

adobo   A marinade sauce, usually made with vinegar, to season or to pickle and preserve a meat.

a dos fuegos   To cook with two fires. This was traditionally done Dutch-oven style, with coals below the pot and placed on the pot lid.

ancho chile   The most popular dried chile in Mexico, it is the dry version of the poblano chile. Typically they are about four and a half inches long and three inches wide.

azumbre   An Arabic liquid measure adopted in Spain. It equals a little more than two liters.

butifarra   A delicate white Catalan-style sausage made from ground pork, spices, and some blood.

chicos   A special kind of corn with small kernels. Toasted while still on the cob, they turn reddish brown and last for a very long time. They were prepared by being shucked, soaked overnight, then cooked for several hours (see Patricia Preciado Martin, *Songs My Mother Sang to Me: An Oral History of Mexican American Women* [Tucson: University of Arizona Press, 1992], p. 16).

chorizo   A spicy orange-colored sausage made with chopped pork, chile, paprika, spices, and garlic. Can be fresh or cured.

cinnamon   *Canela (Cinnamomum verum)*, used in Mexico, is from Ceylon (Sri Lanka). This is preferred to the cinnamon from Vietnam (cassia, *Cinnanomum cassia* or *loureirii*), which is darker and has a hard bark. Cassia is more commonly found in the United States.

comal   A flat ceramic or metal disc used over a flame to cook tortillas, seeds, chiles, and other foods.

emmer   *Triticum dicoccum*. One of the oldest cultivated wheats, also known as *farro*. Today it is primarily grown in Italy, Spain, and Ethiopia.

Galician cabbage   Portuguese cabbage (*Brassica oleracea, Tronchuda* group). Also known as *couve tronchuda*.

granite   Porcelain enamel on ironware.

longaniza   A thin Spanish-style sausage made from minced and marinated pork.

malpica   An otherwise unidentified salad herb. Pinedo mentions it as a standard salad ingredient, along with chervil, tarragon, and green onions.

marmite   A metal or earthenware covered pot with two handles, used for cooking on a hearth or in a stove.

metate   A stone grinding tool used to grind corn, chiles, and other spices. The grinding tool used on the *metate* is usually called a *mano* or *metlapil*.

mole   The Aztec word for "sauce" was *molli*. Generally used to describe a sauce thickened with chiles, nuts, and seeds.

nixtamal   The corn used to make *masa* for tortillas and tamales.

panocha   Same as *piloncillo*, an unrefined cane sugar.

pasilla chile   The dried *chilaca*, also known as a *chile negro*. Usually about six inches long and an inch wide.

pebre   A Spanish sauce with a pimiento base.

picadillo   A shredded meat filling, usually enriched with raisins and olives and spiced with cinnamon.

pipián   A fricassee or a stew with a sauce thickened with squash, pumpkin, sesame, or other seeds.

plate   A cut of beef rarely seen in today's markets. It comes off the beef below the rib and is normally cut into stew meat or ground beef. The only piece of plate normally found today is short ribs.

rape   *Brassica napus.* The leaves are used as a potherb or in salad. The seeds are used like sesame or sunflower seeds or are pressed into canola oil.

tornachile   This is the *güero* chile, a pale-yellow chile.

BIBLIOGRAPHY

Aldrich, Bob. "The Old Mill Stream." *Los Gatos Weekly-Times,* March 27, 1996.

Almaguer, Tomás. *Racial Fault Lines: The Historical Origins of White Supremacy in California.* Berkeley: University of California Press, 1994.

Arbuckle, Clyde. *Santa Clara County Ranchos.* San Jose: Rosicrucian Press, 1973.

Aykroyd, W. R. *The Story of Sugar.* Chicago: Quadrangle Books, 1967.

Baldwin, C. L. "The Peace Keepers." *Santa Clara Forecast,* January 1993.

Bancroft, Hubert Howe. *California Pastoral, 1769–1848.* San Francisco: History Company, 1888.

Belle, Frances. *California Cook Book.* Chicago: Regan, 1925.

Bellefeuille, Sister Julie. Archivist for the Sisters of Notre Dame de Namur. Interview by Victor Valle. Saratoga, Calif., 1992.

Berryessa, Dolores. *Berryessa Family History in California.* Research paper 1152, De Anza College Center for California History, Cupertino, Calif., March 4, 1977.

Blanquel, Simon. *Novisimo arte de cocina; o, Excelente colección de las mejores recetas.* Mexico City: Imprenta Tomás Gardida, 1853.

Bouvier, Virginia M. *Women and the Conquest of California, 1542–1840.* Tucson: University of Arizona Press, 2001.

Brennen, Bonnie. "Cultural Discourse of Journalists: The Material Conditions of Newsroom Labor." In *News Workers: Toward a History of the Rank and File,* ed. Bonnie Brennen. Minneapolis: University of Minnesota Press, 1995.

Camp, Charles. *American Foodways: What, When, Why, and How We Eat in America.* Little Rock, Ark.: August House, 1989.

Clayton, H. J. *Clayton's Quaker Cook Book.* San Francisco: Women's Co-operative Printing House, 1883.

Cleveland, Bess A. *California Mission Recipes, Adapted for Modern Usage.* Rutland, Vt.: Charles Tuttle, 1965.

El cocinero mexicano; o, Colección de las mejores recetas para guisar al estilo americano, y de las más selectas según el método de las cocinas española, italiana, francesa, e inglesa. Mexico: Imprenta de Galván, 1831.

Coit, Lillie Hitchcock. *The Recipe Book of Lillie Hitchcock Coit.* Berkeley, Calif.: Friends of the Bancroft Library, 1998.

Colección recetarios antiguos. Mexico City: Conaculta, 1999–.

Collins, Helen B. "The Tragic Berryessa Family." *Los Fundadores* 11, no. 3 (Summer 1999).

Cooking Receipts: Good in Their Way. [Berkeley, Calif.? 1901?].

[Curtis, Lousie Harrell Peelor]."*I Am So Sick*": *Diary of a Nineteenth Century Housewife.* San Jose: Sourisseau Academy for State and Local History, 1983.

Darby, William J. *Food: The Gift of Osiris.* 2 vols. New York: Academic Press, 1977.

Davidson, Alan. *The Oxford Companion to Food.* Oxford: Oxford University Press, 1999.

Davis, Mike. *City of Quartz: Excavating the Future in Los Angeles.* London: Verso, 1990.

Díaz y de Ovando, Clementina, and Luis Mario Schneider. *Arte culinario del siglo XIX.* Mexico: Fundación de Investigaciones Sociales, 1986.

Elyot, Thomas. *The Castel of Helthe.* London: Thomas Berthelet, 1539.

Esquivel, Laura. *Como agua para chocolate.* Mexico City: Editorial Planeta Mexicana, 1989.

Estate of Lorenzo Pinedo. San Jose County Probate record 74–16838. History San José.

Facciola, Stephen. *Cornucopia II: A Source Book of Edible Plants.* Vista, Calif.: Kampong Publications, 1998.

Fergusson, Erna. *The Mexican Cookbook.* Santa Fe: Rydal Press, 1934.

Fisher, Abby. *What Mrs. Fisher Knows about Old Southern Cooking: Soups, Pickles, Preserves, Etc.* San Francisco: Women's Co-operative Printing House, 1881.

Five Earnest Workers. *Treasures Old and New.* Los Angeles: R. Y. McBride, Art Printer, 1898.

Gabilondo, Aida. *Mexican Family Cooking.* New York: Fawcett Columbine, 1986.

Garcia, Lorie. *Santa Clara: From Mission to Municipality.* Research Manuscript Series 8. Santa Clara, Calif.: Santa Clara University, 1997.

Gibbs, James A. *Shipwrecks of the Pacific Coast.* Portland, Oreg.: Binfords and Mort, 1962.

Gilbreth and Bossue. *Chinese and English Cook Book [Fa ming chung hsi wen ch'u shu pao chien]*. San Francisco: Fat Ming Company, 1910.

Ginger, Bertha. *California Mexican-Spanish Cook Book: Selected Mexican and Spanish Recipes*. Los Angeles: Citizen Print Shop, 1914.

González Sevilla, Emilia, *El fogón del pobre*. Barcelona: Ediciones del Serbal, 1996.

Gratarolus, Gulielmus. *A Direction for the Health of Magistrates and Studentes*. London: William How for Abraham Veale, 1574.

Gvon-Rosenberg, Liora. "Telling the Story of Ethnicity: American Cookbooks, 1850–1900." Ph.D. diss., History Department, State University of New York at Stony Brook, 1991.

Haas, Lisbeth. *Conquests and Historical Identities in California, 1769–1936*. Berkeley: University of California Press, 1995.

Hanna, Eduardus J. *In Harvest Fields by Sunset Shores: The Work of the Sisters of Notre Dame on the Pacific Coast*. San Francisco: Gilmartin Company, 1926.

Hirschler, Mrs. David, comp. *The Council Cook Book: Published by the San Francisco Section of the Council of Jewish Women*. San Francisco: International Printing Company, 1908–9.

Horander, Edith. "The Recipe Book as a Cultural and Socio-Historical Document." In *Food in Perspective: Proceedings of the Third International Conference on Ethnological Food Research, Cardiff, Wales*, ed. Alexander Fenton and Trefor M. Owen, pp. 119–44. Edinburgh: John Donald Publishers, 1977.

How to Keep a Husband; or, Culinary Tactics. San Francisco: Cubery and Company, 1872.

Inés de la Cruz, Sor Juana. *Libro de cocina del Convento de San Jerónimo: Selección y transcripción atribuidas a Sor Juana Inés de la Cruz*. 1979. Reprint, Toluca, Mexico: Instituto Mexiquense de Cultura, 1996.

Johnson, Helen Louise. *The Enterprising Housekeeper*. Philadelphia: Enterprise Manufacturing Company, 1896.

Johnston, Mary Alice. *Spanish Cooking*. Los Angeles: n.p., 1895.

Kovel, Ralph, and Terry Kovel. "Discoveries, Collectibles: Bean There, Done That, So Let's Put a Cork in It." *Los Angeles Times*, November 14, 1998.

Ladies of California. *The California Recipe Book*. San Francisco: Bruce's Printing House, 1872.

Ladies of Sacramento Grace Church. *The Sacramento Ladies' Kitchen Companion*. Sacramento: H. S. Crocker, 1872.

Ladies of the Temple Bazaar. *The Unrivalled Cookbook of Los Angeles*. Los Angeles: Commercial Printing House, 1902.

Landmarks Club, comp. *The Landmarks Club Cook Book: A California Collection of the Choicest Recipes from Everywhere . . . Including a Chapter of the Most Famous Old Californian and Mexican Dishes by Chas. Fletcher Lummis*. Los Angeles: Out West Company, 1903.

Libro de cocina de D. José Moreda, año 1832. Oaxaca, Mexico: Circulo Mexicano de Art Culinario, 1987.

Los Angeles Times. The Times Cook Book No. 2: 957 Cooking and Other Recipes by California Women. Los Angeles: Times-Mirror, [1905?].

———. *The Times Cook Book No. 3: Cooking and Other Recipes by Skilled Housewives*. Los Angeles: Times-Mirror, [1908?].

———. *The Times Cook Book No. 4: Cooking and Other Recipes by Skilled Housewives*. Los Angeles: Times-Mirror, [1911?].

———. *The Times Economy Cook Book No. 5: Practical and Economical Recipes by Skilled Cooks*. Los Angeles: Times-Mirror, 1917.

———. *The Times Prize Cookbook: 453 Good Recipes by California Housekeepers*. Los Angeles: Times-Mirror, [1902?].

Loury, Harriet. *Fifty Choice Recipes for Spanish and Mexican Dishes*. Denver: H. S. Loury, 1905.

Lowenstein, Eleanor. *Bibliography of American Cookery Books, 1742–1860*. New York: American Antiquarian Society, 1972.

Lummis, Charles. *Flowers of Our Lost Romance*. Boston: Houghton Mifflin Company, 1929.

———. *Letters from the Southwest, September 20, 1884, to March 14, 1885*. Ed. James W. Byrkit. Tucson: University of Arizona Press, 1989.

Manual del cocinero y cocinera tomado del periodico literario La Risa. Puebla, Mexico: José María Macías, 1849.

Marshall, Don B. *California Shipwrecks: Footsteps in the Sea*. Seattle: Superior Publishing Company, 1978.

Martínez Peñaloza, María Teresa, "Cocina y farmacia." In *Herencia española en la cultura material de las regiones de Mexico: Casa, vestido, y sustento. XII coloquio de antropologia e historia regionales*, ed. Rafael Diego-Fernández Sotelo, pp. 387–406. Zamora, Michoacán: El Colegio de Michoacán, 1993.

McCaleb, Charles S. *Tracks, Tires, Wires: Public Transportation in California's Santa Clara Valley*. Interurbans Special 78. Glendale, Calif.: Interurban Press, 1981.

McGinnis, R. A. *Beet-Sugar Technology.* 2d ed. Fort Collins, Colo.: Beet Sugar Development Foundation, 1971.

McMahan, Jacqueline Higuera. *Rancho Cooking: Mexican and Californian Recipes.* Reprint of *California Rancho Cooking,* 1983. Seattle: Sasquatch Books, 2001.

McWilliams, Carey. *North from Mexico: The Spanish-Speaking People of the United States.* New York: Greenwood Press, 1968.

Middleton, May. *Recipes from Old Mexico.* San Jose: Melvin and Murgotten, 1909.

Monroy, Douglas. *Rebirth: Mexican Los Angeles from the Great Migration to the Great Depression.* Berkeley: University of California Press, 1999.

Muriel, Josefina. *Cultura femenina novohispana.* Mexico City: Universidad Nacional Autónoma de México, 1994.

Muriel, Josefina, and Guadalupe Pérez San Vicente. "Los hallazgos gastronomicos: Bibliografía de cocina en la Nueva España y el México del siglo XIX." In *Conquista y comida: Consecuencias del encuentro de dos mundos,* ed. Janet Long, pp. 469–79. Mexico City: Universidad Nacional Autónoma de México, 1996.

Narayan, Uma. "Eating Cultures: Incorporation, Identity, and Indian Food." *Social Identities* 1 (1995): 63–86.

Nieto, Blanca. *Cocina tradicional mexicana.* Mexico: Selector, Actualidad Editorial, 1993.

Northrop, Marie. *Spanish American Families of Early California, 1769–1850.* 2 vols. Burbank: Southern California Genealogical Society, 1976, 1984.

Novisimo arte de cocina; o, Excelente colección de las mejores recetas. Philadelphia: Compañía Estereotipográfica de la América del Norte, 1845.

Nuevo cocinero mejicana in forma de diccionario. Paris: Libreria de Rosa y Bouret, 1858. Other editions 1868, 1872, 1888, 1899, 1909.

Obituary of William Fitts. *San Jose Mercury Herald,* March 16, 1916.

Obituary of Encarnación Pinedo. *San Jose Daily Mercury,* April 10 and 11, 1902.

Older, Mrs. Fremont [Clara Baggerly]. Articles from *When Santa Clara Was Young,* a column (372 articles) in the *San Jose Mercury,* 1925, and the renamed *San Jose News,* 1926–27. Nos. 139 and 140, "The Pathfinder's Victim," pts. 2 and 3, ca. 1925; no. 160, "Relics of a Haunted House," ca. May 1, 1926; no. 328, "William Fitts' Omnibus," ca. 1925.

Packman, Ana Bégué de. *Early California Hospitality: The Cookery Customs of Spanish California, with Authentic Recipes and Menus of the Period.* Glendale, Calif.: Arthur H. Clark Company, 1938.

Padilla, Genaro. "Imprisoned Narrative? Or Lies, Secrets, and Silence in New Mexico Women's Autobiography." In *Criticism in the Borderlands: Studies in Chicano Literature, Culture, and Ideology,* ed. Héctor Calderón and José David Saldívar, pp. 43–60. Durham, N.C.: Duke University Press, 1991.

Partridge, John. *The Widowes Treasure, Plentifully Furnished with Secretes in Phisicke.* London: Haviland F. J. Wright, 1627.

Pegge, Samuel. *The Forme of Cury.* London: J. Nicholls, 1780.

Pilcher, Jeffrey. *¡Que Vivan los Tamales! Food and the Making of Mexican Identity.* Albuquerque: University of New Mexico Press, 1998.

———. "Vivan Tamales: The Creation of a Mexican National Cuisine." Ph.D. diss., History Department, Texas Christian University, 1993.

Pinedo, Encarnación. *El cocinero español: Obra que contiene mil recetas valiosas y utiles para cocinar con facilidad en diferentes estilos. Comprendido advertencias y explicaciones aproposito que ponen el arte de la cocina al alcance de todos* [*The Spanish Cook: A Work Containing a Thousand Valuable and Useful Recipes to Cook with Ease in Different Styles. Including Advice and Explanations That Put the Art of Cooking within Reach of Everyone*]. San Francisco: Imprenta de E. C. Hughes, 1898.

———. "Early Days in Santa Clara." *Santa Clara Sunday Bulletin,* June 9, 1901.

Pitt, Leonard. *The Decline of the Californios: A Social History of the Spanish-Speaking Californians, 1846–1890.* Berkeley: University of California Press, 1966.

Plante, Ellen M. *The American Kitchen, 1700 to the Present: From Hearth to High-rise.* New York: Facts on File, 1995.

Preciado Martin, Patricia. *Songs My Mother Sang to Me: An Oral History of Mexican American Women.* Tucson: University of Arizona Press, 1992.

Recetario de doña Dominga de Guzman, siglo XVIII. San Ángel, Mexico: Sanborn's, 1996.

Reichl, Ruth. "California Cuisine: The Tradition of the New." *Los Angeles Times,* November 7, 1991.

Reinstedt, Randall A. *Shipwrecks and Sea Monsters of California's Central Coast.* Carmel, Calif.: Ghost Town Publishers, 1975.

Robinson, W. W. *Los Angeles from the Days of the Pueblo: Together with a Guide to the Historic Old Plaza Area Including the Pueblo de Los Angeles, State Historical Monument.* San Francisco: California Historical Society, 1959.

Ruiz de Burton, María Amparo. *The Squatter and the Don.* Ed. and intro. by

Rosaura Sánchez and Beatrice Pita. 1885. Reprint, Houston: Arte Público Press, 1992.

Sánchez, Rosaura. *Telling Identities: The Californio Testimonios.* Minneapolis: University of Minnesota Press, 1995.

Secretaría de Educación Pública y Instituto Nacional de Antropología e Historia. *Atlas cultural de Mexico: Gastronomia.* Mexico City: Grupo Editorial Planeta, 1988.

Smith, Mary G. *Temperance Cook Book: For the Benefit of All Housekeepers.* San Jose: Mercury Book and Job Printing House, 1887.

Southworth, May. *101 Mexican Dishes.* San Francisco: Paul Elder, 1906.

Spearman, Arthur Dunning. *The Five Franciscan Churches of Mission Santa Clara, 1777–1825: A Documentation.* Palo Alto, Calif.: National Press, 1963.

Strehl, Dan., ed. and trans. *The Spanish Cook: A Selection of Recipes from Encarnación Pinedo's "El Cocinero Español."* Pasadena, Calif.: Weather Bird Press, 1992.

Super, John C. "Libros de cocina y cultura en América latina temprana." In *Conquista y comida: Consecuencias del encuentro de dos mundos,* ed. Janet Long, pp. 451–68. Mexico City: Universidad Nacional Autónoma de México, 1996.

Taylor, Fred G. *A Saga of Sugar: Being a Story of the Romance and Development of Beet Sugar in the Rocky Mountain West.* Salt Lake City: Utah-Idaho Sugar Company, 1944.

Theophano, Janet. *Eat My Words: Reading Women's Lives through the Cookbooks They Wrote.* New York: Palgrave, 2002.

Thompson and West. *History and Atlas for Santa Clara County.* San Francisco: Thompson and West, 1876.

Torres de Rubio, Vicenta. *Cocina michoacana.* Zamora: Imprenta Moderna, 1896.

Tuñón Pablos, Julia. *Women in Mexico: A Past Revealed.* Austin: Institute of Latin American Studies, University of Texas Press, 1999.

Valle, Victor, and Mary Lau Valle. *Recipe of Memory: Five Generations of Mexican Cuisine.* New York: New Press, 1995.

Viviano, Frank. "The Lost Paradise of the Californios." *San Jose Mercury News West Magazine,* June 16, 1985, pp. 7–11, 24–26.

Weaver, William Woys. "Additions and Corrections to Lowenstein's *Bibliography of American Cookery Books, 1742–1860.*" *Proceeding of the American Antiquarian Society* 92 (1982): 363–77.

———. "More Additions to the Lowenstein *Bibliography of American Cookbooks, 1742–1860*." *Journal of Gastronomy* 6, no. 2 (Autumn 1990): 103–12.

Williams, Jacqueline B. *The Way We Ate: Pacific Northwest Cooking, 1843–1900*. Pullman: Washington State University Press, 1996.

Yamada, Kakichi. *The Sense of Cooking: Talks on Culinary Arts by K. Yamada and B. Shibuya*. San Francisco: Aoki Taisedo, 1928.

Zelayeta, Elena. *Elena's Famous Mexican and Spanish Recipes*. San Francisco: Dettner's Printing House, 1944.

———. *Elena's Favorite Foods, California Style*. Englewood Cliffs, N.J.: Prentice-Hall, 1967.

———. *Elena's Fiesta Recipes*. Los Angeles: Ward Ritchie Press, 1952.

———. *Elena's Lessons in Living*. San Francisco: Dettner's Printing House, 1947.

INDEX

Accommodation Line Omnibus, 22
acemitas, 61
achicora, ensalada de, 130
adobos, 193; *para carne de cerdo*, 149;
    de España, 148; *para lomos*, 150; *para*
    pollos, 150; *de rango*, 149; *seco*, 151; *para*
    viandas, 149; *para viandas de almendras*
    y nueces, 150
agua de anis, 159
albericoques: helados de, 170; *mermelada*
    de, 181–82
albóndigas: a la alemana, 94; *de cataluña*,
    95; *delicadas*, 81; *a la española*, 57, 94;
    españolas a la alemana, 96; *de frailes*, 58;
    a la italiana, 95
albondiguillas: fritas, 69; *de merluza*, 71
alcachofas, 116; *ensalada de patatas con*
    fondos de, 131; *en vinagre*, 116
almendras: adobo para viandas de almen-
    dras y nueces, 150; *arroz en leche de*,
    159–60; *crema de*, 169; *jarabe de hor-*
    chata a la española, 175; *leche de*, 176;
    salsa de aceitunas y almendras, 153;
    sopladas, 159
almonds: cream, 169; marinade, with
    walnuts, for meats, 150; milk, 176;
    puffs, 159; rice in almond milk, 159–
    60; sauce, with olives, 153; syrup,
    Spanish-style, 175
Anglo conquest of California, 3, 15, 20
anise: cakes, 179; water, 159

apricots: marmalade, 181–82; sherbet,
    170
arroz: guisado a la española, 117; *en leche*
    de almendras, 159–60; *pastel de, a la*
    argentina, 134; *pudin de*, 185
artichokes, 116; potato salad with arti-
    choke bottoms, 131; in vinegar, 116
asados: de buey, 96; *de buey a la mexicana*
    en asador, 97; *de carnero*, 97; *de lechón*,
    98; *de pecho de ternero*, 97
asparagus, 91
aves: en almendrado, 83; *asadas en pipián*
    de pepitas de melon y almendras, 82;
    capon al horno, 84; *escabeche de gallina*,
    85; *en estofado*, 83; *fricasa a la española*,
    86; *gallinas rellenas*, 87; *en mole gallego*,
    82; *picadillo de*, 91; *en pipián de ajonjoli*,
    81; *relleno blanco para aves asadas*, 144;
    relleno de patatas para aves asadas, 147.
    See also codornices; guajolotes; pichones;
    pollos

bacalao: en aceite y tomate, 72; *a la biz-*
    cáina, 74; *chiles rellenos de*, 123; *a la*
    española, 72; *con pan rallado y queso*,
    73; *con queso*, 74; *en salsa blanca*, 74;
    en salsa de chile, 73; *en tomate y chile*
    verde, 73
bain-marie, 109n2
Bancroft, Hubert Howe, 2
barbacoa, 98

poultry, selection of, 52

preserves, 53–54; candied orange, 167; green-chile sauce for, 157; green fig, 168; quince, 169; squash, 169; sweet orange, 168; tomato, 143; watermelon (the queen of Cuba), 167. *See also* jellies; marmalades

puchero, 60; *de cola de buey*, 60

puddings: Chonita's, 189; Diana's, 186; fruit, 186–87; Julieta's, 187; Leticia's, 188; Little Carmen's, 187; Mrs. W. Fitts's bread, 189–90; orange, 186; rice, 185; Rosita's, 188; sauces for, 157–58; Spanish-style, 164; young ladies', 185

pudines: de arróz, 185; *capirotada, o pudin a la española*, 164; *de Carmencita*, 187; *de Chonita*, 189; *de Diana*, 186; *de frutas*, 186–87; *de Julieta*, 187; *de Leticia*, 188; *de naranja*, 186; *de pan por la señora W. Fitts*, 189–90; *de Rosita*, 188; *salsas para*, 157–58; *de señoritas*, 185

puerco: adobo para carne de cerdo, 149; *asado de lechón*, 98; *cochinillo en adobo*, 104; *costillas de puerco fresco con setas*, 105; *patitas de cerdo en adobo*, 102; *relleno para lechón asado*, 146

punches: red-wine, 184; rum or Scotch-whiskey, 184–85; Spanish-style, 184

quail: pie, 90; Spanish-style, 84

quince: best marmalade, 179–80; preserve, 169

rabbit: in chile sauce, 108; French-style jugged, 107

race, 5, 11

racial identity, 14–15

Ramona, 13

Rancho Las Uvas, 20

Rancho Santa Teresa, 20

Rancho San Vicente, 20

raspberries: jelly, with lemon, 173; syrup or cream, 174

ratafia, 190

recipe transmission, 24

red currants: jelly, 173; pie, 182

refried beans, 132

rellenos: blanco para aves asadas, 144; *para costillas*, 145; *dulce*, 144; *para ganso*, 145; *para lechón asado*, 146; *de patatas para aves asadas*, 147; *para pato asado*, 145; *para pescado*, 147; *para pichones asados*, 146

remolacha, ensalada de, 131

ribs: à la mode, 99; stuffing for, 145

rice: in almond milk, 159–60; Argentine-style casserole, 134; pudding, 185; stewed Spanish, 117

roasts: beef, 96; lamb, 97; Mexican-style grilled beef, 97; missionary-style pot, 101; suckling pig, 98; veal breast, 97

rolls: English-style, 61; semolina, 61

royal cream, 182

Ruiz de Burton, María Amparo, 3

Sacramento Ladies' Kitchen Companion, 26

salads: beet, 131; cabbage, 129; chicory, 130; crab, 131; cucumber, 129; dressing for, 155; lettuce, 129; mustard dressing for, 155; potato, with artichoke bottoms, 131; shrimp, 130

salsas: de aceitunas y almendras, 153; *el adorno de una mesa*, 151; *bechamel con setas para ostras*, 154; *de chiles verdes para conservas*, 157; *de chile verde*, 156; *empiñada para pollos*, 85; *para ensaladas*, 155; *escabeche*, 86; *española*, 152; *a la española para pulpa de carne de buey*, 154; *general*, 153; *de mostaza para ensaladas*, 155; *nogada*, 151; *de nueces para todo*, 152; *para pescados*, 153; *picante de chile colorado*, 156; *para pollos*, 154; *de tomate a la española*, 155

DESIGNER Nola Burger
TEXT 8.5/14 Caecillia Roman
DISPLAY Mrs. Eaves; Chaparral Bold; Interstate
COMPOSITOR Integrated Composition Systems
PRINTER AND BINDER Friesens Corporation